Third Eye Awakening

Open Your Third Eye Chakra for Higher Consciousness, Spiritual Healing, Self-Care, and Mindfulness

Travis Hemingway

Copyright 2023 Travis Hemingway – ALL rights reserved!

The contents of the book may not be reproduced, duplicated or transmitted without the direct written permission from the publisher or author.

Under no circumstances will any legal responsibility or blame be held against the publisher or author for any reparation, damages, or monetary loss due to the information herein, either directly or indirectly.

Legal Notice:

This book is copyright protected. This is only for personal use. You cannot amend, distribute, sell, use, quote or paraphrase any part or the content within this book without the consent of the author or publisher.

Disclaimer Notice:

Please note the information contained within this document is for educational and entertainment purposes only. Every attempt has been made to provide accurate, up-to-date and reliable information. No warranties of any kind are expressed or implied. Readers acknowledge that the author is not engaging in rendering legal, financial, medical or professional advice. The content of this book has been derived from various sources. Please consult a licensed professional before attempting any techniques outlined in this book.

By reading this document, the reader agrees that under no circumstances is the author or publisher responsible for any losses, direct or indirect, which are incurred as a result of the use of the information contained within this document, including but not limited to, --errors and omissions, or inaccuracies.

Table of Contents

Words From The Author   1
Introduction   2
Chapter 1 Significance of the Chakras   6
  The Concept and Significance of Chakras   6
    Why Should You Learn About the Chakras?   8
      Muladhara: The Root Chakra   9
      Swadhisthana: The Sacral Chakra   11
      Manipura: The Solar Plexus Chakra   13
      Anahata: The Heart Chakra   14
      Vishuddhi: The Throat Chakra   16
      Agna: The Third Eye Chakra   19
      Sahasrara: The Crown Chakra   19
Chapter 2 Third Eye Chakra—Seat of Knowing and Intuition   22
  What Is the Third Eye Chakra?   22
    The Color Associated With the Third Eye Chakra   23
    The Element Associated With the Third Eye Chakra   24
    The Mudra Associated With the Third Eye Chakra   25

The Third Eye Chakra in Different Schools of Thought 25
- Hinduism 25
- Buddhism 28
- Taoism 28
- Egyptian Mythology 29

A Scientific Understanding of the Third Eye Chakra 30
- The Pineal Gland 30
  - Ancient Wisdom Related to the Pineal Gland 32
- The Pituitary Gland 33

Learning to Embrace the Idea of the Third Eye Chakra 35

Chapter 3 Is Your Third Eye Chakra in Alignment? 37
- Symptoms of a Blocked Third Eye Chakra 37
- Symptoms of an Aligned Third Eye Chakra 44

Chapter 4 The Path to Knowing, Intuition, and Awakening 51
- The Difference Between Knowledge and Knowing 52
- What Is Spiritual Awakening? 56

Chapter 5 Practices That Can Help Align Our Third Eye Chakra 67
- Diet and Third Eye Chakra Alignment 67
  - Foods That Help Us on Our Third Eye Chakra Awakening Journey 72

The Importance of Yoga in Third Eye Awakening 73
Yoga Asanas for Third Eye Chakra Awakening 75
   Balasana (Child's Pose) 75
   Ardha Pincha Mayurasana (Dolphin's Pose) 77
   Garudasana (Eagle Pose) 79
Chapter 6 Practices to Strengthen Your Intuition 82
Signs of Heightened Intuition 84
Issues Faced During This Process 86
How Can We Strengthen Our Intuition? 87
   The Use of Essential Oils 88
   Meditating With Crystals 90
   Third Eye Meditation Techniques 90
      The Practice of Sun Gazing 91
      Trataka Dhyana (Gazing Meditation) 91
      Third Eye Chakra Visualization 93
   Pranayama Techniques for Third Eye Chakra Awakening 93
      Nadi Shodhana Pranayama 96
      Bhramari Pranayama 98
      Yogic Breathing 99
Hakini Mudra 99
Dream Journaling 100
Harnessing the Healing Power of Nature 102
Other Techniques to Awaken Our Third Eye Chakra 103

Chapter 7 The Importance of Chanting for Third Eye Chakra	106
The Importance of Bija Mantras	106
The Significance of "Om"	107
Benefits of "Om" Chanting	107
How to Do a Chanting Meditation	108
The Power of Affirmations	109
Making the Most of This Journey	110
Conclusion	112
Thanks for reading!	116
References	117

Words From The Author

Hey, it's Travis. Thank you so much for giving me a chance to make an impact in your life. I feel its my *mission* to help guide anyone and everyone who is looking for an answer. I find it important that I share what I've learned on my journey thus far. Hopefully, by doing so, you all won't have to feel as lost as I once did. That's all for now and I hope I'm able to help.

As a thanks for your support, I have a **FREE** gift for you. Just scan the code below.

Introduction

The truth isn't taught; it's realized. –Kierra C.T. Banks

When people think of spiritual enlightenment, they feel intimidated and overwhelmed. In fact, many believe that it's a fancy term invented by a few to dupe others when it comes to their time, money, and agency. This last one—agency—is the most important one. When we talk of spiritual paths, we usually talk in terms that imply giving up on our own plans for ourselves and surrendering to something higher than us. For those of us who believe in the superiority of willpower, it can be really disorienting to think of surrender in terms of anything but giving away our power to the unknown. The result is that, even though we find ourselves intrigued by the concept of spiritual awakening, we don't understand how to reconcile these ideas with the largely material lives that we lead.

It's true that spiritual awakening is a term that gets bandied about a lot. There's also an overabundance of spiritual gurus who claim to be able to do much of the work for you. It's ironic that the path to knowledge and enlightenment is often strewn with confusion and disenchantment. As someone who's embraced the spiritual path in their own lives, I know that it doesn't have to be this way. This book is my attempt to give you back your power. More accurately, it's about making you see the power that already resides within you.

This is a book about third eye awakening. For those who have an idea about *chakras*, the third eye is an important—albeit mysterious—destination for many. I would argue that it isn't a destination as much as an important milestone in an endless journey (more on this later), but I understand the value that this journey holds for all of us. After all, the third eye is known as the seat of intuition, knowledge, and enlightenment. The interesting thing about third eye chakra awakening is that, if you're actively seeking this path and reading up on it, you might be closer to your spiritual destiny than you think. After all, the urge to seek the truth is a powerful indicator that you're on your way to it.

The challenges that arise on the path to spiritual awakening are largely internal in nature. More specifically, these challenges are about discovering and sticking to our own truth when the world outside us tries to trick us on a daily basis. Reality is bearable to most of us because it comes with the false promise of truth. We go through each day convinced that this is all there is to it, that we've figured out how to live and survive, and that the life we've built is worth it. Without this conviction, we'll move through life disoriented and unmotivated.

However, there are those amongst us who refuse to believe that they've known and experienced everything there is. There are those whose inner voice hasn't quite been dulled by the din of the real world. There are those who want to test the limits of what they think they know. This is a book for seekers like you.

Through this book, we'll understand the third eye chakra in detail. We'll get to know what this chakra stands for, its significance in spiritual awakening, and its effect on our intuitive abilities. We'll also dispel some of the common myths that are connected to the third eye chakra. We'll dedicate a large part of the book to understanding how our intuition can help us in both material and spiritual ways and how we can sharpen it.

Also, for those of us who aren't immersed in the spiritual traditions, it can be difficult to understand when our third eye chakra is blocked or out of alignment. Therefore, we'll learn how to check in with ourselves and pay attention to the relevant symptoms. The last part of the book will be focused on developing a practice that we can incorporate in our daily lives. This practice includes lifestyle changes, yogic and meditation-based exercises, and chanting and affirmations. The aim will be to identify practices that we can do on a regular basis to sharpen our intuition and awaken our third eye.

At its core, this book is about understanding our own selves at a deeper level. It's about knowing who we are and having faith in that knowledge. What does it mean to truly know the worlds inside and outside you? What does intuition mean to you and how can it help you navigate this world? What does awakening mean to you? Why is the spiritual path worth pursuing to you? These are only some of the questions that we'll dive deeper into in this book.

Another aspect of this journey that is often overlooked is the effect that this deep knowing can have on our lives. (And yes, there's a difference between "knowing" and "knowledge"—more on that in Chapter 4!) Without balance and perspective, it can be very difficult to find our footing in the material world after undergoing a third eye awakening. On the one hand, it can be a surreal and ecstatic experience to finally understand yourself and the world. On the other hand, we might struggle to carry on with our daily responsibilities or connect with those around us once we understand the true nature of reality. Not only can this hamper our quality of life, but it can also keep us from connecting deeply with the world around us. So, in this book, we'll be discussing the importance of maintaining balance between our material and spiritual realities.

No one can be a better guide for yourself than you. That being said, we can all struggle with knowing and believing in ourselves every now and then. Think of this book as a path that gently leads you back to yourself.

Chapter 1
Significance of the Chakras

Most of us live our lives firmly rooted in the physical or material realm, and there's nothing wrong with that. However, the problem is that many of us go through life disconnected from both our internal and external worlds. Since our bodies and minds are more or less adept at helping us navigate the physical world, we don't often tune in to these processes and understand them at a deeper level. The concept of *chakras*—though rooted in ancient Hindu beliefs—can be challenging to understand for most of us. Also, even though the concept itself has gained popularity in the Western world over the years, there are still a few misconceptions around it that need to be cleared.

For most of us, the concept of chakra awakening can sound either too esoteric or too difficult to put into practice. This belief can keep us from using this wealth of knowledge to our advantage. In this chapter, we'll introduce ourselves to the concept of chakras and also understand how it can help enrich our daily lives.

The Concept and Significance of Chakras

The word *chakra* originates from Sanskrit, and it translates to "wheel." To understand chakras in detail, we need to understand the concept of the "subtle body." The subtle body—also known as the energetic body—is like a reservoir for our *prana* or "life force." Notably, the concept of life force isn't limited to the Hindu school of thought. Known also as chi or qi, our life force energy keeps us energetic throughout life. People who are low on this life force energy might feel unwell or "out of balance" even if they can't seem to find any physical issues with themselves. Our life force is what makes us feel physically, emotionally, and spiritually aligned with ourselves at all times.

Even though we cannot "see" or perceive our subtle body, it can affect almost every aspect of our lives. This is why it's important that this life force energy flows freely through our subtle body. This is where chakras come in. They act as "energy centers" for the subtle body. In general, energy flows through our subtle body through pathways known as *nadis*. These *nadis* converge at certain points throughout the body, and these points are known as chakras.

While different schools of thought have clashing opinions when it comes to the actual number of chakras, most are aligned with the existence of the "six plus one" chakra system, which is what we're going to be adhering to in this book. According to this system, there are seven chakras within the subtle body. Though these are not actually located in the physical body, we can find physical representations of these chakras that make it easier for us to understand their impact on our material lives.

Why is the knowledge of chakras important for us? Before we answer this question, let's also understand that you don't need to believe in a specific religion to resonate with this concept. Even though it has its roots in Hinduism, this concept can be used by anyone who wants to understand themselves at a deeper level, improve their physical, mental, and spiritual well-being, and even experience spiritual awakening.

Why Should You Learn About the Chakras?

Everything in our world is governed by energy. Without energy, the Earth would be lifeless and so would we. Also, since energy can neither be created nor destroyed, we need to ensure that we receive energy in the form that's most useful for us at a particular moment. This life force energy powers our material as well as spiritual reality. So, it's important to keep it unblocked and free-flowing at all times.

The chakras offer a different dimension to our physical reality. They help us understand our bodies through an energetic lens. Specifically, you can understand why certain parts of your physical body aren't working well. Chakras can also tell us why we feel depleted in certain areas of our lives, or how we're preventing ourselves from fulfilling our potential. Here, it's also important to note that the knowledge of chakras shouldn't be taken as a substitute for professional medical advice, and that you should always consult a professional if you're dealing with physical, mental, or emotional issues. That being said, having a deeper understanding of our energetic body can widen our perspectives and make us feel more connected with ourselves.

Let's now discuss each of the seven chakras in detail.

The first three chakras—also referred to as the *lower* chakras—are related to the physical realm. Even though they're known as lower chakras, they're not any less significant than the four *higher* ones. In fact, if these chakras are not in alignment, it's impossible to progress on your spiritual journey. In the next section, we'll also discuss the spiritual aspects of these "physical" chakras.

Muladhara: The Root Chakra

This chakra forms the foundation of our physical reality. In the physical body, it's said to be located at the base of the spine. Symbolically, this chakra is depicted as a four-petaled lotus. The four petals represent the air, water, fire, and earth elements, respectively. These four petals emanate from a square that holds an inverted triangle, which signifies our connection to the earth. This chakra is represented by the earth element and the color red.

Since this chakra is the foundation of our physical body, it is closely related to stability, strength, health, and physical well-being. When we have an active and balanced root chakra, we identify with our physical body in a healthy manner. We might experience a sense of dynamism, enthusiasm, and liveliness in the way we navigate our physical reality. Mentally, the root chakra also relates to feelings of stability and security. In other words, an aligned root chakra could make us feel sure of ourselves and our place in the world.

The root chakra deals with our most basic needs, which include food, shelter, and safety. So, if we're feeling confident about our ability to earn money and save it for the future, and if we feel safe in our physical reality, our root chakra is likely aligned. Similarly, if our root chakra is balanced, we feel stable and secure in our current relationships.

Let's now look at this chakra from a spiritual lens. In ancient yogic traditions, we have a concept known as *kayakalpa*, which roughly translates to "renewal of the body." Literally speaking, *kaya* refers to the body, and *kalpa* refers to the unit that describes one entire cycle of the cosmos. In other words, when we measure the time period between the creation and destruction of the universe, it's known as kalpa. So, when we try to increase the life span of our bodies, we're not only trying to improve our physical health and longevity. We're also trying to test our spiritual potential. After all, using our body to transcend the limits of our physical reality is a core aspect of spiritual practices like yoga. When our root chakra is balanced, we can slow down the deterioration of our body, which can help improve our spiritual prowess as well.

How do you know if your root chakra is out of balance? Physically, you might suffer from weak bones, poor strength, lack of balance, as well as issues related to the colon or urinary tract. Since you don't feel confident in your ability to master your physical reality, you might also feel lazy, unmotivated, and inertial. If you're feeling more fatigued than usual—and you've ruled out any other underlying causes—there's a chance that your root chakra might be out of balance.

This is a good time to clear another common misconception related to chakra-cleansing. Many people use the terms "closed" and "open" chakras. The idea is that a closed chakra might block energy from flowing through it, while an open chakra will facilitate the free flow of the prana. This is somewhat misleading. Ideally, we want our chakras to be "balanced" or "aligned," instead of open. This is because, when our chakras are too open or active, they might create issues within our systems. For example, when our root chakra is too active, it might lead to an overidentification with our physical reality. For example, if you feel like you're obsessing a lot over your finances and physical health to the point that you're not paying attention to other aspects (such as the spiritual dimension) of your life, there's a chance that your root chakra is too active. Similarly, if you find yourself getting too rigid or stubborn, your root chakra might be out of balance.

Swadhisthana: The Sacral Chakra

The sacral chakra can be seen as the center through which creative, sexual, and reproductive energy flows. In the physical body, it's located just below the navel. It's also known as the "abode of the self," because it's related to how we see ourselves. Symbolically, this chakra is depicted as a six-petaled lotus, which represents the cycles of death, birth, and rebirth. This chakra is represented by the water element and the color orange.

The sacral chakra is often seen as the seat of the Divine Feminine energy. It's important to note that the masculine and feminine energies mentioned in spirituality have nothing to do with our biological sex or even our gender. No matter how we identify in the physical world, all of us have a mix of both masculine and feminine energies within us. The Divine Feminine energy is related to sexuality and sensuality, pleasure, creativity, and procreation. This energy—connected as it is with water—is affected by the power of the moon.

When our sacral chakra is aligned, we can feel confident in our sexual and creative abilities. It can also help us reach the often-elusive *flow state*, where we don't need to exert too much effort to be our true selves. When our sacral chakra is balanced, it's a good time not only for physical creation, but also for creative expression of all kinds.

When this chakra is out of balance, however, we can suffer from various issues. Physically, it might lead to issues in the lower back, urinary tract, and reproductive system. Emotionally, it can lead to self-worth issues, which might lead to repression of our sexual and creative tendencies. Instead of experiencing a flow state, we might feel like we're stuck or in some way or another—much like a writer's or artist's block. We might not feel motivated enough to create and express ourselves. When we're not in touch with our feminine energies, we might struggle to nurture ourselves and others. What happens when these energies are in overdrive? In such cases, we might find ourselves dealing with obsessive tendencies, lust, and overindulgence.

From a spiritual lens, this chakra can enhance our abilities of creation to the extent of creating Divine entities. Please note that the creation of a Divine entity isn't something that should be undertaken lightly. It's not even possible for all of us to participate in such a process. Nevertheless, this is an intriguing concept that helps us understand the spiritual aspect of an otherwise "physical" chakra. In this context, a Divine entity is one whose energy is of a higher—and purer—quality than humans. Anyone who has gone through the process of creating something knows how much it can take from you. When it comes to giving birth to other entities, the amount of energy required is immense. Therefore, the most important thing is to be able to create another, higher entity without losing your life or sense of self. This can only happen if all your chakras are aligned.

Manipura: The Solar Plexus Chakra

This chakra is the seat of our self-esteem and confidence. Physically, it's located in the upper abdomen. This is a chakra that maintains what has been created by the *swadhishthana* chakra. It's represented by the color yellow and the fire element. Symbolically, the solar plexus chakra is represented by a ten-petaled flower.

To understand how our solar plexus chakra affects us, let's look at people who are confident of themselves. Such people are usually warm, generous, and compassionate. Since they don't need to prove themselves to anyone else, they don't resort to insecure behaviors. They're also confident about starting new ventures or meeting new people. When our self-esteem is high, we don't get fazed by others' negative opinions. In order to maintain what has been created, we need to have faith in ourselves.

When our solar plexus chakra is out of balance, it can manifest in the form of physical issues in the stomach. People who regularly suffer from digestive issues might have an unbalanced solar plexus chakra. Similarly, issues such as heartburn and ulcers could also result from this imbalance. Emotionally, this lack of balance can lead to a sense of powerlessness and insecurity. People who suffer from low self-esteem might have trouble taking charge of their lives. They might also avoid social situations and any scenario where they might be in the spotlight.

Also, since we don't feel like we're in control of our lives, we might start focusing too much on others. This can lead to feelings of insecurity that stem from comparing our lives with others. In extreme cases, we might even have to contend with feelings of intense envy and greed. On the other end of the spectrum, an unbalanced chakra might also lead to displays of aggression and pride. You might act out by pulling others down or by dismissing other people's opinions in your life. You might even struggle to draw the line between being assertive and aggressive. While these behaviors might seem like a display of confidence, they're actually signs of insecurity.

Spiritually, the solar plexus chakra is related to movement and stillness. This is the only place in the subtle body where all the 72,000 *nadis* converge and redistribute themselves. This means that this chakra is instrumental in the distribution of energy (prana) throughout the body. As we move from this chakra to the four higher chakras, we also make a journey from movement to stillness.

Anahata: The Heart Chakra

This chakra is sometimes seen as the bridge between the physical and spiritual realms. This is also the seat of pure unconditional love. Physically, it's located just above the heart in the center of the chest. Thus, it affects not only the heart but also the lungs and chest.

Symbolically, the heart chakra is depicted by a figure of 12 petals containing an upward-facing triangle intersecting with a downward-facing triangle. This symbol shows that we're now moving from the lower chakras to the higher ones—as the downward-facing triangle signifies the physical realm while the upward-facing one signifies the spiritual realm. This chakra is represented by the air element and the color green.

When our heart chakra is aligned, we experience love toward ourselves and others. This is important because true love cannot be experienced outside of ourselves. An aligned heart chakra also helps us be empathetic toward others. This means that we can respect other people's experiences and believe them, even when those experiences are different from ours. In its purest state, the heart chakra helps us experience and live our lives according to Divine love.

When the heart chakra is out of balance, it can lead to physical problems like heart ailments, asthma and other lung diseases, and even issues related to our weight. Emotionally, it can disrupt our relationships with ourselves and others. In this case, fear takes the place of love. When we're scared of ourselves, we don't allow ourselves to experience life fully. We don't sit with ourselves to understand who we are, what we want, and what makes us feel whole. In extreme cases, we might suffer from self-hatred as well. After all, there is a thin line between fear and hatred, as we've seen all too often in the world.

When it comes to our relationships with others, we might find ourselves acting from a place of insecurity. When meeting strangers or people whose circumstances and backgrounds are different from ours, we might react with fear and even hostility. Even in our intimate relationships, we might struggle to communicate and act with love. A blocked heart chakra can also lead to intense feelings of isolation and loneliness. When our heart chakra is aligned, we have no trouble connecting with others, even during difficult times. In fact, we might begin to see ourselves as a part of an intricate web of life. A blocked heart chakra, on the other hand, might make us feel misunderstood and out of place in this world.

There's another way in which this lack of balance can manifest in our lives. Sometimes, we might suffer because we don't know how to love ourselves before loving others. In other words, we might not know how to prioritize and heal ourselves before we get into relationships of any kind. We might also struggle to draw clear boundaries with those we love and be honest about our needs and expectations. If you find yourself giving too much of yourself without getting anything in return, your heart chakra might be out of alignment.

To understand the spiritual significance of this chakra, we need to understand what *anahata* means. In Sanskrit, *anahata* means unstruck or unhurt. The unstruck sound is one without reverb, which signifies absolute serenity and balance. In order to bring our heart chakra into balance, we need complete steadiness of intellect. However, our intellect might not be useful if it isn't accompanied by emotions. Here, again, we see how the balance between intellect and emotion can help us explore the spiritual dimensions of the heart chakra.

Vishuddhi: The Throat Chakra

The fifth chakra in the subtle body is the seat of authenticity and expression. Physically, this chakra is located in the throat region. Symbolically, the chakra is represented by sixteen petals, each of which is inscribed with a vowel from the

Sanskrit language. This figure is said to signify the importance of communication in keeping this chakra aligned. This chakra is represented by the space element and the color blue.

When this chakra is balanced, you will have no difficulty communicating your needs to others. Not only will you be able to speak confidently and passionately, but you will also become a better listener. People with balanced throat chakras understand the sacred importance of communication in all interactions. Thus, they don't use their words carelessly and also pay attention to what others are trying to tell them. When they speak, we can get a glimpse of their conviction and compassion—both through their words and the meaningful silence.

An aligned throat chakra also makes it easier for us to live our truth. We become comfortable with who we truly are, and we also gain courage to live our lives aligned with our authentic selves. Usually, the path to authenticity is beset with resistance from people, especially those who are close to us. An aligned throat chakra gives us the courage to express ourselves clearly and stick to our beliefs even when faced with challenges. Last but not least, an aligned throat chakra makes us feel grateful for our lives. When we experience gratitude, our capacity for joy also increases.

When the throat chakra is blocked, we might suffer from problems related to our throat, mouth, teeth, gums, and voice. It can also be related to feelings of inadequacy and issues with self-expression. People who don't believe in themselves often have trouble expressing their needs in front of others. Aside from this, they might also follow others without questioning them or holding them accountable. Such people might appear unsure of themselves. They might have trouble speaking clearly and honestly and might not even be good listeners. In extreme cases, people with blocked throat chakras might even resort to lies and gossip while communicating with others.

On the other end of the spectrum, a blocked throat chakra might also manifest as overconfidence and aggression during conversations. People who speak too much without letting others get a word in, or those who always want conversations to go their way, usually have problems related to the throat chakra. Also, when our throat chakra is out of balance, we might struggle to count our blessings. Without gratitude, we might focus excessively on the challenges we have to face, thus making us sad and bitter. When this chakra is blocked, we might also have to deal with mood disorders like depression.

Spiritually, a lot of the understanding of this chakra's abilities comes from the deity who is primarily associated with it. In Hindu traditions, Lord Shiva is seen as *adiyogi*—the first yogi. Also known as *Neelkanth* (the blue-throated one), he's depicted as someone whose throat glows blue. There are various interpretations of this phenomenon, but one of the most popular ones—with respect to spiritual awakening—is the idea that the practice of yoga allowed Shiva to achieve a state where his throat chakra was activated and he was able to attract disembodied beings toward himself. Think of it as the removal of a veil that sets the material and spiritual worlds apart. An awakened throat chakra helps us get in touch with the mystique that surrounds us, but that we're unaware of in our daily lives. This state is also seen as one in which we attain mastery over our emotions, so that we can use them to help us instead of making our lives more challenging.

Agna: The Third Eye Chakra

The sixth chakra is known as the seat of intuition and knowing. We'll be discussing this chakra in great detail in the next chapter, so I'll move on to the last chakra in this chapter.

Sahasrara: The Crown Chakra

If the sixth chakra is all about understanding the true nature of reality, the seventh—and last—chakra is about experiencing joy like never before. Physically, this chakra is located at the top of the head, also known as the crown. The symbol for this chakra is a thousand-petaled lotus. There's no element that represents the highest chakra. When it comes to colors, some people believe that it can be represented by violet. Most, however, believe that this chakra is represented by the color white, which signifies the combination of all the colors of the rainbow, thus referring to the universal energy of this chakra.

Since this chakra is connected to all the other chakras, it can have an effect on every part of our body. Because it is located on the top of the head, it has a direct impact on our head and spinal system. Emotionally, this chakra is related to unconditional joy—even ecstasy. In this state, one experiences the bliss of uniting with the Higher Consciousness.

While this is also known as the chakra of enlightenment, the term "enlightenment" in this context is not so much the ability to know reality as it is the ability to experience a state that is entirely beyond the physical. This is also why there's no path that leads us from the sixth to the seventh chakra. In other words, you cannot really *do* something to initiate an awakening of this chakra. If anything, this stage asks for complete surrender to the infinite—almost like an ability to enter into an eternal dance with the unknown.

When this chakra is blocked, we might suffer from headaches and problems related to our hearing and vision. At the same time, we might become acutely aware of the conflicts in the world. Instead of embracing everything with an open heart, we might find ourselves feeling skeptical and narrow-minded. Instead of surrendering to the unknown, we might become overly attached to our physical reality.

To be honest, there's no "material" parallel to this chakra, but we can understand this state through certain concepts. For example, this state is symbolized by the crescent moon that is seen on Shiva's head. This crescent moon signifies the bliss and intoxication that we can taste when we're in this state. The main aim for people who are fortunate enough to experience this state is to not get so immersed in it that a physical existence becomes impossible for them.

Before we move on to the next chapter, here are a few more things to understand about chakra awakening. While the underlying principles remain the same, everyone's path looks different. An important aspect of a spiritual journey is to identify what the journey means to us and to gain a deeper sense of understanding about yourself in the process. As long as you keep that in mind, you can make this journey your own.

Another thing to keep in mind is that your chakra awakening journey might not be linear. Of course, it's important to achieve a certain level of alignment before we can move on to the higher chakras. However, the journey itself can follow a route that isn't conventional. Also, just because your chakra is aligned once, it doesn't mean that it cannot be blocked in the future. In fact, depending on our physical, mental, and emotional state, we might have to start working on our foundations every now and then. This doesn't mean that the progress we've made on the journey so far doesn't count. All it means is that we should reframe how we see spiritual progress. Even when it seems like we're starting from scratch or moving backward, we're getting closer to the most authentic version of ourselves—and that is what makes this journey worth it.

In the next chapter, we'll familiarize ourselves with the third eye chakra in detail.

Chapter 2
Third Eye Chakra—Seat of Knowing and Intuition

Have you ever experienced déjà vu in your daily life? Maybe you were going about your day and suddenly experienced a strong feeling of having seen or being a part of this exact situation before. Or, you've been a part of situations where you simply *know* what to do or how to react even though you have no real context for it. No matter how logical or rational you might think you are, many of us have a brush with our inner knowing and intuition. We might dismiss it or we might lean into it, but most of us go through life getting a sense of what isn't physically visible or obvious to us.

If we don't understand these abilities properly, we might lose out on opportunities to enhance our lives through them. We might also erroneously believe that such abilities are only available to the select few, which is not the case. Of course, it takes time and practice to align our third eye chakra, but we cannot do that unless we truly understand the concept in the first place. In this chapter, we'll delve into the third eye chakra and its implications for our lives.

What Is the Third Eye Chakra?

This is the sixth chakra in the subtle body. It's also the last chakra that can be actively worked on through a dedicated spiritual practice. While these chakras aren't actually located in the physical body, their "physical" locations can help us understand their place in our spiritual journey. The third eye is located in the center of our forehead, exactly four inches behind the center of the eyebrows. This chakra is symbolized by two lotus petals, in the middle of which is an inverted triangle. The inverted triangle is said to represent enlightenment. The center of the symbol displays the *bija* (seed) mantra known as *Om* (more on this later).

The Color Associated With the Third Eye Chakra

The third eye chakra is associated with the color indigo. Why is indigo used as a symbol for this chakra? This is because indigo is seen as a deeply spiritual color in numerous traditions across the world. In general, it is seen as a color that can boost our awareness of ourselves and the world around us. This way, it can be used to raise our consciousness and access other states of being that aren't usually available to us. This is also why this color is usually associated with the practice of meditation.

Indigo is a color of fairness and impartiality as well. In other words, this color usually helps us see things *as they are* and not as we would like them to be. The third eye chakra works on similar principles as it encourages insight and intuition. This color is also related to wisdom and intuition.

Another way of looking at indigo is as a combination of red and blue, both of which have great significance in spirituality. Indigo is seen as a color of balance between the fiery energy associated with red and the calmness associated with blue. So, not only does this color represent vitality and dynamism, but it also signifies tranquility. Without tranquility, it's impossible to become aware of our true nature.

Last but not least, the color indigo is related to transitions—both from life to death and from one plane of existence to another. This is important because an aligned third eye chakra helps us perceive things that are beyond this plane of reality. This color is also seen as a symbol of "escaping the material plane."

The Element Associated With the Third Eye Chakra

The third eye chakra is associated with "light." This requires a bit of clarification. Since this chakra is associated with "insight," the concept of vision becomes very important here. The two "physical" eyes are used to perceive the material world, while the third eye helps us see the world beyond this material plane. Now, even in this world, we can only see something if it interacts with light. In spiritual terms, light stands for true understanding, clarity, and insight.

When we look at light as an element, it's one that travels faster than sound. Also, light has an interesting relationship with the universe. For example, the light of the sun takes roughly eight minutes to reach the earth. Similarly, when we receive light from different stars in the universe, we're seeing them not as they are in this moment, but in the moment when they were illuminated by this light. When we draw a parallel with the third eye chakra, we realize our ability to look clearly not only in the past or future, but also across dimensions.

Another—closely related—school of thought believes that there's no element associated with this chakra, as it does not really deal with anything belonging to this plane of existence. This is why the term *avyakta* is used in relation to this chakra. *Avyakta* stands for "that which is without a form" or "that which cannot be expressed."

The Mudra Associated With the Third Eye Chakra

In ancient traditions such as Hinduism, Buddhism, and Jainism, mudras play a huge role in helping us balance our prana. They are usually combined with meditation and yoga. While mudras can involve our entire body, most of them are *hasta* mudras, also known as hand gestures. Different mudras are used for different purposes. These can help in improving our physical, emotional, and spiritual processes. Mudras are also an integral part of our spiritual awakening process.

The mudra associated with the third eye chakra is known as the *hakini* mudra. *Hakini* means "power" or "rule" in Sanskrit, and is related to the goddess Hakini in the Hindu tradition. Goddess Hakini personifies both the hemispheres of the brain, and is known to represent inner knowing, intuition, and imagination—all aspects of the third eye chakra.

The Third Eye Chakra in Different Schools of Thought

Many cultures and traditions have embraced the third eye as an important aspect of the spiritual journey. Let's take a closer look at these cultures.

Hinduism

In Hinduism, the third eye is closely related to Lord Shiva. The word *ajna* comes from Sanskrit, and it stands for "foremost" as well as "command." In other words, the third eye is the prominent seat of intuition and awareness. Also, this chakra is located in the head and can act as a control center for many physical, emotional, and spiritual processes. The word *ajna* (pronounced *agya*) also means "beyond wisdom." In Hindu customs, a *tika* or *tilak* is placed on a person's forehead—usually after the morning prayers—where the third eye is supposed to be. The *tilak* is a small—usually red—mark placed on the third eye chakra. When the chakra is gently pressed and covered by *tilak*, it's supposed to preserve the energy of the third eye chakra. Also, it is said to help with concentration and wisdom as we tackle the demands of the day.

Also known as *urna*, the third eye is first seen in Lord Shiva. According to the myth, Shiva's right eye signifies the sun and his left eye signifies the moon. The third eye is the one that can see beyond reality and illusion. It's also seen as a signifier of destruction and protection. Shiva is known to protect his followers from evil, and he's also seen as the Destroyer. In fact, it's said that when Shiva opens his third eye, it'll lead to the destruction of the world as we know it. This can be hard to deal with for someone who doesn't understand the spiritual significance behind this.

The myth goes that *Kamadeva*—the god of lust—shot an arrow at Shiva's heart while he was on his path to become the *Adiyogi*. When this happened, Shiva opened his third eye and burnt Kamadeva to ashes. As you might imagine, this can seem like a scary interpretation of the power of the third eye.

However, we need to understand the symbolism behind this. Here, lust refers to any desire we might have in our lives. As humans, it's next to impossible to live life without any desires. When we desire something, we feel motivated to work toward it. It's also known as ambition or longing—concepts that urge us to pursue things in life. Without desire, we might as well not have a purpose. The thing is, these desires are usually—if not always—material in nature. In many cases, we don't even know if we truly want what we are chasing in our lives.

Desires usually come from a place of inadequacy. As long as we want the next thing, we cannot be focused on what we have. Desires are limitless, which means we can spend an entire lifetime feeling like we're not enough. This is separate from having a purpose that is true to your soul. For Shiva, his purpose was to achieve mastery over the practice of yoga, which would help him understand the true nature of reality. Any desires that stood in his way didn't come from an external source but within himself. We need to pay attention to this part.

When we begin our spiritual practice, it's easy to attribute our distraction to external circumstances. The truth is, we're the ones who are unintentionally creating obstacles on our own path. So, when Shiva "destroys" Kama, he's actually destroying everything within himself that's keeping him from perceiving the truth of this world and the world beyond. This is why the third eye is seen as something that makes us see inside ourselves. In other words, whatever we're looking for is already inside us—and this journey simply makes it easier for us to embrace this truth.

We'll discuss more about the connection between the third eye and our intuition in the fourth chapter.

Buddhism

According to Buddhist beliefs, the third eye is extremely important in helping humanity to end its suffering. According to this school of thought—which is similar to the Hindu school in many ways—an aligned third eye helps raise the consciousness of the practitioner. This helps us move beyond the physical plane and look at reality through the "eye of the soul."

In many *thangka* paintings—which are sacred Tibetan Buddhist paintings—the deities usually have a third eye on their foreheads. It symbolizes that, in any enlightened being, the third eye is open and becomes the "wisdom eye."

Of the three main teachings of Buddha—discipline, meditation, and wisdom—the third eye alignment is related to the process of gaining wisdom. According to the teachings, it's possible to gain wisdom only through the "Right View," which means being able to perceive the ultimate—rather than the relative—truth.

In other words, the ability to perceive reality as it is—and not as it is shown to us because of our own shortcomings—is directly related to the awakening of the third eye chakra.

Taoism

The concept of prana isn't limited to Hinduism and Buddhism. In Taoist traditions, the vital life force is known as qi. Just like pranayama is the practice of controlling and working with the prana, the "microcosmic orbit" is a Taoist meditation technique that helps control the flow of energy through the subtle body. This practice is deeply connected to the concept of the third eye.

The third eye in Taoist practices is related to intuition, spiritual awareness, and inner vitality. Just as with Hindu and Buddhist traditions, Taoist beliefs also place a lot of importance on energy work, mindfulness, and meditation to align our third eye chakra.

Egyptian Mythology

In Egyptian mythology, the symbol—known as the Eye of Horus—is linked to the third eye. This eye is related to the Egyptian god Horus, who was the god of war, sky, and protection. This Eye of Horus is seen as a symbol of prosperity, good health, power, and protection. It's also related to rejuvenation, healing, and rebirth. Often seen as the representation of the sun, this symbol is connected to illumination, which takes us back to the connection between light and the third eye.

It's also depicted as the "all-seeing eye." This symbol can be seen on ancient Egyptian artifacts and even tombs. An interesting attribute of this symbol is that—when placed over the image of the human brain—its different parts correspond to the parts of the brain that are responsible for sensory regulation. As our senses help us perceive the world, the Eye of Horus is responsible for the expansion of our perceptive qualities.

A Scientific Understanding of the Third Eye Chakra

It's true that the third eye chakra is a deeply spiritual concept. However, there has been a growing interest in the scientific working of this chakra in recent years. While this concept still faces resistance from many researchers, there are some who want to gain an understanding of the third eye from a scientific perspective. The parts of the brain that are associated with the third eye are pineal gland, hypothalamus, and pituitary gland. These are usually associated with mental health, vision, sleep, and spiritual awareness.

The Pineal Gland

The pineal gland is an endocrine gland located in the epithalamus region of the brain. It's a pea-sized gland that looks like a pinecone, and it is responsible for regulating our circadian rhythms by secreting and regulating melatonin. This gland works in conjunction with a region in the hypothalamus that records how much light our eyes are receiving at any point.

Melatonin is a hormone that is secreted based on how much darkness our eyes receive. In other words, when we sleep at night, our body produces melatonin. During the day, melatonin production decreases so that we are alert and active. All of us have an internal clock that works according to our circadian rhythms. When our sleep-wake cycles are regular, our circadian rhythms are normal. This ensures good physical and mental health, and it also prevents stress and anxiety from taking over our lives. When we don't sleep properly or sleep at the wrong time, we mess with our natural circadian rhythms. Not only does this make us feel more tired than usual, but it can also affect our moods and energy levels in a more permanent way over time.

Apart from regulating our sleep-wake cycles, the pineal gland also has an impact on our reproductive and sexual health, immune health, and aging-related processes. In terms of physical and physical health, our third eye—or pineal gland—has a huge impact on us. For example, healthy melatonin levels and a proper sleep-wake cycle can affect our cardiovascular health as well as cognitive functions. You might find yourself feeling sadder or moodier if you haven't slept well for a few days. If this becomes a pattern, you might even have to deal with mood disorders like anxiety and depression.

Research also suggests that the pineal gland might affect our bone health over time. When melatonin production reduces in our body, we become susceptible to bone disorders like osteoporosis. Since the pineal gland responds to light, some people might also suffer from seasonal affective disorder if they live in regions where winters are long and dark.

Our pineal gland can be affected both by issues in the hypothalamus and by excessive calcification (deposit of calcium on the pineal gland). When the pineal gland malfunctions, it has an impact on our circadian rhythms. Over time, other symptoms might start showing up, such as

- Osteoporosis, especially in postmenopausal women
- Changes related to ovulation, fertility, and menstruation
- Nausea
- Tremors

- Headaches
- Mental health issues
- Issues with sense of direction

Ancient Wisdom Related to the Pineal Gland

Many ancient spiritual traditions have referred to the pineal gland as the third eye. For some, this is because the pineal gland is located close to the visual cortex and is directly related to the interplay of light and darkness. Also, philosophers have believed that the pineal gland helps not only with physical but also spiritual vision—helping us "see" internal images more clearly.

Over the years, it has been called "the seat of the soul." In 2000, clinical psychiatrist Rick Strassman wrote about a possible effect of the pineal gland on our physical, mental, and spiritual health. In his book *DMT: The Spirit Molecule*, he talked at length about the pineal gland and its ability to secrete dimethyltryptamine (DMT), which is a strong psychoactive compound usually found in certain plants and animals. Since it is psychoactive in nature, it usually causes hallucinatory effects in people who consume it. According to Strassman, the pineal gland can secrete this compound on its own, especially during major events such as birth and death. In this way, it can be instrumental in enhancing our life force as part of a spiritual awakening. It's important to note here that we have yet to find conclusive scientific evidence when it comes to a significant presence of DMT in our pineal gland.

However, a review was conducted to understand how the relationship between light, third eye, and the pineal gland can affect our physical and mental health. The review concluded that the pineal gland is much more complex than initially thought, and it has an effect not only on the secretion of important hormones like melatonin and serotonin, but also on DMT. This way, it seems to have an impact on various neurological and psychiatric conditions as well (Gheban et al., 2019).

The significance of the pineal gland is also present in *chronomedicine*. Chronomedicine is derived from an understanding of how circadian rhythms work and how diseases develop due to the disruption of these cycles. According to the alternative medicine system of Ayurveda, our bodies and minds are regulated by three *doshas* (the sources of problems)—*vata*, *pitta*, and *kapha*. Since our doshas are intricately linked with our circadian rhythms, the pineal gland plays an important role in chronomedicine. Not only that, but the timing of our medicines is also dependent on these circadian rhythms (Kumar et al., 2018).

The Pituitary Gland

The pituitary gland is also pea-shaped and is seen as being physically closer to the location of the third eye. This is an important gland because it's instrumental in the secretion of most major hormones. Since it plays such a vital role in regulating our hormones and in creating balance within the body, it plays an important role in aligning our third eye chakra.

To understand the importance of the pituitary gland and hypothalamus in terms of the third eye chakra, we can look at children. You might have noticed that the heads of children need special protection. In fact, certain areas of their heads are extremely tender, and these areas are where the pituitary gland and hypothalamus reside. When you're holding an infant, for example, you might be advised to gently hold the tender part of their head for protection.

Now, we know that children are extremely intuitive by nature. They seem to have a natural curiosity not only for the physical world but also for the world that we don't perceive easily. In fact, their questions might give you an idea about their capacity to wonder about anything and everything at the same time. It's believed that this happens because their third eye is aligned at the time. Their consciousness is also raised and they are more susceptible to energies that adults cannot usually pick up. One theory which explains this is related to the different kinds of waves that our brain emits.

For example, when we feel sad, anxious, or angry, our brains emit *beta* waves. When we feel happy and calm, on the other hand, our brains emit *alpha* waves. It's said that infants and young children emit a higher number of alpha waves because their pituitary and hypothalamus region is tender. As we grow older and this region becomes less tender, the number of alpha waves emitted by our brains decrease, thus blocking our intuitive abilities.

The third kind of wave is known as *gamma* wave, which can only be experienced by people who meditate for long periods of time and reach a state of *samadhi*. During *samadhi*, the practitioner experiences complete ego dissolution. In other words, there's no difference between the person's individual consciousness and the Universal Consciousness. In some cases, samadhi might even lead to the person leaving their physical body for good.

These three waves are primarily responsible for the different states we experience in our daily lives as well as during our spiritual awakening process. In order to sharpen our intuition, we need to intensify the emission of alpha waves in our brain.

Learning to Embrace the Idea of the Third Eye Chakra

In general, the third eye chakra is related to intuition and deep knowing. However, these two words don't always do justice to the scope of this chakra. Since this chakra is the second to last chakra we encounter on our spiritual journey—and indeed the last one that we can gain real mastery over—it can seem intimidating to anyone who first encounters its powers. Even in our daily lives, we sometimes get a glimpse of what it means to truly *know* something, but those moments are rarely strong enough to convince us to go deeper. What's more, if we talk about these instances with our loved ones, it's likely that they'll either dismiss us or ridicule us. Even if they don't, they might be more worried than impressed at our "abilities." Of course, some cultures are more open to these ideas than others. Even so, most individuals face challenges when it comes to the awakening of their third eye chakra.

In a largely rational world, it can be difficult to have faith in our intuitive abilities. This is because, by nature, our intuition belongs only to us. We don't need external validation or energy to sharpen it. For this very reason, however, we might have trouble working on these abilities. The biggest challenge that can arise on this path is that of skepticism. Of course, it can be daunting to keep going when others around us question our path, but it can be even more difficult to suppress our own doubts as we progress along this journey.

Another issue that arises on this journey is our tendency to rationalize whatever we're feeling and experiencing on this journey. For example, when you suddenly get a premonition or "see" something ahead of its time, do you talk about it confidently or do you attempt to make light of the matter? When you begin to notice certain patterns and synchronicities in your life, do you pay attention to what they might be telling you, or do you keep dismissing them as coincidences that you are reading too deeply into?

The thing is, we're so often told that intuition or gut instinct is inferior to reason. After a while, we start believing this to be an irrevocable truth. Before we begin our journey to awakening our third eye chakra, however, it's extremely important that we rid ourselves of any hesitation regarding the path. Don't get me wrong: It's completely normal to experience some doubt now and then, especially in the initial phases of the journey. That being said, you need to be open to the journey and everything that comes with it. Most importantly, you need to understand *why* you're starting this journey and why it matters to you. Without this conviction, it will be very difficult to align your third eye chakra.

Chapter 3
Is Your Third Eye Chakra in Alignment?

Have you ever been through a period in your life where you felt extremely cynical about the world in general? Maybe you struggled to have faith in yourself and your abilities. Maybe you felt disconnected from the people around you. Or, you were surrounded by people who believed in you but you struggled to trust them. Since the third eye chakra brings clarity, insight, and awareness to ourselves and the world around us, it can be extremely disconcerting when this chakra is out of alignment.

If you're not aware of the possibilities associated with this chakra and the issues arising from a blocked chakra, you won't be able to progress on your spiritual journey. Let's understand these aspects in detail in this chapter.

Symptoms of a Blocked Third Eye Chakra

To understand the symptoms of a blocked third eye chakra, we need to be aware of its effects on our life. Since this chakra is closely related to vision and hearing and is located on the forehead, these are the areas that are most affected by any blockage in the chakra. Some of the physical symptoms of a blocked third eye chakra are

- Poor or blurred vision, or general problems with eyesight
- Hearing issues
- Blocked sinuses
- Headaches and migraines
- Hormonal imbalance
- Metabolism-related issues
- Dizziness
- Seizures
- Issues related to the spinal cord and nerves

As always, it's extremely important to first get yourself checked by a medical professional to rule out any medical concerns. Don't assume that these issues could be the result of any blockage in your third eye chakra.

A blocked third eye also manifests in the form of emotional and mental symptoms. Let's look at some of these:

- You might start suffering from memory issues. Since our third eye is intricately linked to **memory and concentration**, you might find yourself struggling to remember things clearly and accurately. At the same time, you might find it difficult to focus on important matters.
- If you find yourself getting **more anxious** than usual, you might be suffering from a blocked third eye chakra. In general, anxiety occurs when we feel uncertain about ourselves and our lives. The thing is, life is uncertain for all of us. We need faith in ourselves to navigate its many highs and lows. When our third eye is blocked, doubt and confusion take the place of faith, which can lead to an exacerbation of anxiety symptoms.

- A blocked third eye chakra might also lead to **greater confusion** in life. Let's face it: Most of us go through life confused by the various choices available to us. As the world gets more chaotic and saturated with information, it's normal to feel confused and overwhelmed. That being said, if you find yourself feeling more confused than usual, you might be suffering from a blocked third eye chakra. A good way to understand this is by paying attention to the things that you previously thought you had clarity on. Were there certain choices that you didn't have a lot of trouble making? Have those choices somehow become more daunting recently? If your answer is yes, that means that your third eye chakra might be out of alignment.
- The third eye chakra also affects the realm of **sleep and dreams**. We've seen the close relationship between this chakra and the pineal gland—which is responsible for our sleep-wake cycles. When this chakra gets blocked, we might suffer from disrupted sleep schedules. In extreme cases, we might even have to struggle with insomnia. A blocked chakra might also manifest in the form of nightmares. If your sleep schedule has changed drastically or the quality of your sleep has diminished, you might need to align your third eye chakra.
- When aligned, the third eye chakra can also make us feel like we're in control of our dreams (more on this soon). When blocked, it might seem like our dreams are overtaking our lives and coming in the way of our daily duties. If you notice a heightened **tendency to daydream**, you might be struggling to balance your third eye chakra.
- It's perfectly normal to feel out of sync with yourself every once in a while, just like it's okay to feel disconnected from your internal and external world.

Nevertheless, if you're **struggling to either find your purpose or relate to it** for an extended period of time, you might need to check in with yourself. Your vision doesn't need to be grand or "important," but it needs to make sense to you. As important as it is to deal with the daily challenges of life, it's equally important to have something greater to aspire to. Without that, we might feel as if we're simply going through the motions of life.

- This symptom is related to the one above. If you feel like you're **stuck in life** and that you're **lacking inspiration**, you might be struggling with a blocked third eye chakra. An aligned third eye chakra can help us see our path clearly, and it can also give us the confidence needed to work on our skills and goals. If you find yourself falling into a rut that you can't seem to get out of, you might need to work on clearing your third eye chakra.
- The third eye chakra is also the seat of **imagination and creativity**. When this chakra is blocked, your imagination might feel severely limited. In other words, you might struggle to get new ideas or work on any of them. You might even have difficulty in critical and divergent thinking.
- One way of knowing if your imagination is adversely affected is to check how you deal with uncertainty and scarcity. For example, creative people usually know how to make the best of limited resources or time. In fact, the truly creative might even embrace limitations as a way to enhance their creativity. This can be seen in the famous Oulipo tradition, through which French-speaking mathematicians and writers used limitations to create intriguing works. A popular example is *A Void*, a novel by Georges Perec that has been written entirely without the use of the letter "e."

- As you can imagine, that's a difficult feat to achieve in our daily written communication, let alone while penning a novel. However, these artists believed that the restrictions they placed on their writing would make them better and more creative writers. Contrast this attitude with that of someone who constantly complains about not having the proper tools or conditions needed to create. If you fall into this category, you might have to work on aligning your third eye chakra.
- Since this chakra is related to the realm of possibilities, it brings with it a sense of optimism and hope. Here, I'm not talking about toxic or forced positivity, where you need to trick yourself into believing that everything is or will be okay. When we gain true clarity of ourselves and our lives, we *know* that things will be okay because we're on the right path. In other words, we're able to see our struggles and setbacks in a more balanced and positive light. When this chakra is blocked, however, the darkness of the world can threaten to engulf us. Your third eye chakra might be blocked if you feel **extremely pessimistic** most of the time, or if you keep asking yourself, "What's the point?"
- Since this chakra is related to sleep and calmness, a chakra that is out of balance might result in various **mood disorders**. Disturbed sleep cycles can also contribute to greater stress and anxiety. In some cases, you might have to deal with depression and paranoia as well. You might also feel hopeless about the world. In other cases, you might start expecting the worst of the world. If you find yourself struggling with your mental health, consult a professional to become familiar with your underlying thought patterns.
- If you want to check in with your third eye chakra, try to examine your beliefs. Have they become **overly logical**

or rational in the recent past? Do you try to "make sense" of everything that happens to you or to others around you? Are you eager to provide rational explanations for anything that seems difficult to explain or out of the ordinary? If you do, your third eye chakra might be blocked. On the other end of the spectrum is a tendency to get overly emotional in various scenarios. Whether we're detached from our emotions or immersed in them, there's a chance that we aren't seeing things clearly—which is an indication of the chakra being blocked.

- While spiritual beliefs might not come naturally to many of us, we can certainly be open to them. If nothing else, we should have the ability to deal with questions that cannot be answered easily without feeling threatened by them. By their very nature, spiritual questions are designed to make people uncomfortable. That's completely okay. The problem arises when we **shut down any conversation related to spirituality**. If we run away from anything that isn't completely material, we might need to work on our third eye chakra.

- How are your relationships with others around you? Are you comfortable having deep and meaningful conversations with the people in your life or do you prefer keeping things as **superficial** as possible? Of course, it's not possible or advisable to engage in such conversations with strangers or people you haven't formed a strong bond with. That being said, if you struggle to do this with anyone in your life—especially those who are receptive to such ideas—you might have a blocked third eye chakra. In general, if you have trouble trusting people or getting close to them, your third eye chakra might be blocked.

- When our third eye chakra is blocked—or when we've just started on our chakra awakening journey—we might feel **more irritated or angrier** than usual. If you have previously done a lot of work on yourself and even forgiven people for hurting you, it might surprise you when those feelings resurface. You might suddenly find yourself reliving past memories—especially the painful ones—and dealing with the unpleasant emotions that accompany them. Similarly, you might find yourself becoming less patient with people and their faults. In extreme cases, you might even act **arrogant, entitled, or superior to others**. When our third eye chakra is aligned, our ego begins to dissolve and we feel connected to others. When it's blocked, our ego takes center stage in our life. You might even become **stubborn and rigid** when it comes to your beliefs.
- Since the third eye chakra deals with our intuition, a blocked chakra can seriously **mess with our intuitive abilities**. In some cases, you might have trouble trusting your gut. You might feel lost and directionless and struggle to make sense of what your inner voice is telling you. Even if your instinct tells you something, you might be compelled to dismiss it. In other cases, you might have to contend with feelings of impending doom. In other words, your gut might be telling you that something is wrong, even though you might not be able to put your finger on it.

The most obvious symptom of a blocked third eye chakra is that you feel as if you don't have any access to the wisdom around and within you. This lack of access can manifest in many ways, especially in the form of anger, frustration, and confusion. Also, it might seem like these symptoms are limited to a blocked eye chakra. However, you might experience these symptoms even when you've started aligning your chakra. We'll discuss this aspect further in the next chapter.

Symptoms of an Aligned Third Eye Chakra

To understand how the third eye chakra affects us, we need to pay closer attention to the various symbols that are associated with it. For example, its bija mantra *Om* is said to be the aural embodiment of the Divine Consciousness or of the entire cosmos. In this way, it stands for the energy of non-duality. Similarly, the visual representation of this chakra is the two-petaled lotus. The two petals also signify that the third eye chakra takes us away from the concept of duality. In some interpretations, the two petals are said to stand for Lord Shiva and Goddess Shakti. While Shiva symbolizes destruction and transformation, Shakti stands for both creativity and dissolution. Do you see how their attributes perfectly complement each other? Not only that, but Shiva and Shakti also stand for the Divine Masculine and Divine Feminine energies, respectively. Yet another school of thought pays attention to two words *Ham* and *Ksham* that are written on the two petals of the lotus. These words are also said to signify Shiva and Shakti, respectively. Sometimes, Shiva is said to be the spiritual representation of the pineal gland while Shakti signifies the pituitary gland.

Together, they embody the concept of non-duality—much like the third eye chakra—by showing us that there is no real separation between the different kinds of entities or energies. In fact, the devotee is no different from the object of devotion. The energy of Universal Consciousness runs through everything and everyone, and an aligned third eye chakra makes it possible for us to see it.

Seen through the lens of the original Hindu, Taoist, and Buddhist traditions, the ultimate aim of third eye chakra awakening is to recognize this Universal consciousness running through everyone—in other words, to recognize the divine energy that flows through the entire cosmos.

Let's discuss how an aligned third eye chakra can affect our physical, mental, and emotional energies.

When it comes to physical symptoms, the most important effect is related to the pineal and pituitary glands and the hypothalamus. When the third eye chakra is balanced, these parts of the body work optimally, thus leading to better hormonal balance. Since the pituitary gland is the "master gland," it controls the release and regulation of various hormones. On one hand, a balanced third eye chakra can control physical processes such as metabolism, reproduction, and growth. On the other hand, it's also related to the release of important hormones such as vasopressin and oxytocin. While vasopressin plays a vital role in maintaining blood pressure, water balance, and overall kidney health, oxytocin is popularly known as the "love hormone." This hormone—which is released when a mother bonds with their child, when we hug or cuddle with someone we love, or when we take part in social bonding exercises—helps us feel good about ourselves and the people we interact with. When our third eye chakra is aligned, we experience these "happy" feelings in a more intense manner. As we can see, even the physical effects are closely linked to mental and emotional effects.

Here are a few mental and emotional symptoms of a balanced third eye chakra:

- **Improved clarity of thought and expression**: When the third eye chakra awakens, we can finally see things clearly. There is little to no confusion in our thoughts and in the way we express ourselves. One of the best ways of checking this is by thinking about something that confuses you. This could be a situation that you don't have clarity on or a person you're unsure about. Chances are, even with all the information available to you, you might be struggling to get a clear sense of your own feelings about the issue. Once your third eye chakra awakens, revisit the situation and you'll know exactly how you feel about it. Not only that, but you'll also be able to express your thoughts clearly to others.
- **Better concentration and memory**: An aligned third eye chakra will make it easier for you to focus on the present. You'll also be able to remember things and people as they were and not as you would like them to be. Memory is an extremely fickle thing, and it can sometimes be complicit in helping us avoid harsh truths. For example, you might find yourself glossing over the details of something unpleasant that happened in the past, just so that you can feel comfortable in the future. Our (lack of) memory can protect us every now and then, but it's not useful for anyone who wants to truly grow and heal.
- **Sharpened intuition and true insight**: Intuition and insight are closely linked concepts. Our intuition tells us something "more" than what the facts are. Also known as our "gut feeling" or instinct, it's something that cannot be readily explained but is extremely powerful. For example, someone who has worked in the same industry

for a long time is usually in a better place to make intuitive decisions than someone who has just entered it. Similarly, some people are better at sensing how others are feeling, even when things are not explicitly stated. In some cases, time and experience might lead to a better sense of intuition. However, in others, intuition could also be related to new and strange people or situations. For example, you might meet someone for the first time and realize that their "vibes are off." Our intuition might not always give us the answers we're looking for, but it can certainly prod us to investigate further. Insight, then, is related to intuition because we can only arrive at an insight if we're willing to go beyond surface-level explanations of a situation. An insight is something that, when uncovered, might seem extremely obvious. At the same time, it stays hidden from plain sight unless we're willing to do the work of understanding something or someone deeply. An awakened third eye chakra sharpens our intuition and helps us gain deeper insight.

- **Heightened imagination and creativity**: An awakened third eye chakra stimulates our imagination and makes us feel more confident in our creativity. You might find yourself more enthusiastic about trying new things. You might even come up with novel solutions to problems you have been stuck on forever. If your mindset shifts from being fixed to being growth-oriented, there's a good chance that your third eye is coming into balance. What's more, you might even start noticing connections between seemingly disparate things after your awakening.
- **Greater confidence in being yourself**: We've seen that an awakened throat chakra gives us the confidence to live an authentic life. We start expressing ourselves in a way that aligns with who we are and what we stand for. However, the throat chakra stage is still a few steps away

from knowing the true nature of reality. When the third eye chakra is balanced, not only do we know ourselves but also the world we reside in. This makes it that much easier to inhabit this world as our true selves. Even when we're expressing ourselves, we don't feel threatened by what others think of us. In many ways, an aligned third eye chakra helps us get rid of our deepest fears.

- **Reduced stress and anxiety**: In some cases, our third eye chakra awakening can lead to clairvoyance (more on this in the next chapter), which can help us see beyond the physical or into the future. In both cases, this added knowledge can certainly help ease our anxiety. Even without gaining clairvoyance, however, the clarity and understanding that accompanies this process can help reduce stress to a great extent. After all, we now understand what matters and what doesn't, and we also know what is worth investing our energy in. Even when we're faced with uncertainty, we know what we want and what our strengths are. We're also less likely to feel intimidated by the unknown as we're able to glimpse at the cosmic picture.

- **A deeper sense of connection with the world**: We can only connect with others to the extent that we're connected to ourselves. If we aren't comfortable in who we are, we might have trouble forming healthy relationships with others. Not only that, but constant stress and anxiety can even lead us to burnout. This is when we struggle to form meaningful connections with others. Feeling isolated or misunderstood can only add to the sense of disconnect we experience. When the third eye chakra is balanced, we first come into connection with ourselves. This sense of harmony then radiates outward and affects anyone who interacts with us. At a deeper level, we can even begin to sense that boundaries are artificial and that there are no real differences between us. When we begin to see everyone as divine beings, we don't give in to the "us versus them" mentality. Consequently, it becomes much easier to connect with people from different backgrounds and beliefs.

- **Heightened sense of perception**: We interact with the world through our five senses. Normally, these senses are somewhat muted or become overwhelmed as the result of dealing with way too many energies on a regular basis. The third eye chakra helps our senses regain their power. Suddenly, you might find yourself having a greater appreciation for the world around you. You might notice things that you would otherwise have ignored. As your perceptive abilities increase, you might also become sensitive to changes in your environment. Not only does this open up the world's riches to us, but it also helps us pick up on other people's energies more accurately. For example, highly sensitive people (HSPs) usually have the ability to pick up on the energies of their surroundings, which can be a superpower but can also overwhelm them every now and then. The trick lies in finding a balance within ourselves.

- **A highly positive outlook on life**: Again, positivity in this context doesn't imply that we are deluded about our lives. In fact, it's the clarity we achieve during and after the awakening process that makes it easier for us to see things in a positive light. For one, we become more receptive to the world around us, which means we understand that grief and pain also have their place in this world. We don't see grief, pain, and loss as things that subtract from the world but as those that add to its richness. Also, since awakening can increase our capacity to love, we begin to accept the hardships and the conflicts in our lives with greater ease. Perhaps most importantly, a balanced third eye chakra helps us stay curious at all times. We become eager to experience the world in all its glory, and no two days stay the same after this. Instead of feeling like we're running on autopilot, we can finally feel like we're in control of our lives. This control, however, isn't about stubbornly micromanaging our destiny, but about surrendering ourselves to the will of the universe.

- **An experience of calmness and bliss**: As I've mentioned before, we might experience anger and frustration at the beginning of the third eye activation journey. This can certainly seem unsettling, but the important thing to remember is that this is part of the process. Think of it this way: If you want to see clearly through a lens, you need to make sure that it is clean and devoid of any dust. In the same way, if you want to gain clarity and understanding, you need to remove anything that could obstruct your vision. Anger, frustration, and grief might seem like hindrances when they first show up on our journey, but they're extremely important to deal with before we begin to experience the calm and bliss associated with the third eye chakra. Once the chakra is balanced, we might find that the same situations that once used to trigger us don't affect us as much, or even at all. Instead, we experience a sense of calm washing all over us. What's more, this sense of bliss has nothing to do with the "external" world. This means that—for perhaps the first time ever—we're the only ones responsible for our happiness.
- In this chapter, we've familiarized ourselves with the symptoms of a blocked and a balanced third eye chakra. In the next chapter, we'll dive deeper into the spiritual aspects of a third eye chakra awakening.

Chapter 4
The Path to Knowing, Intuition, and Awakening

Before we begin our third eye chakra awakening journey, we need to understand what it means to truly awaken. Since the terms "chakras," "awakening," and "spirituality" are having a moment, there are many self-proclaimed gurus who are ever ready to accompany us on this journey. Many of them might even promise to lead the way, and all we have to do is follow them. This can be very confusing for anyone who is just beginning their journey. On one hand, all of us look for guidance when we're embarking on an intense and unconventional journey. We want to seek out people who have traversed this path before and who might have some wisdom to impart to us. In most spiritual traditions, there is the concept of a teacher or mentor who prepares their students for the journey.

On the other hand, it's really difficult to know the intentions of a person before accepting them as your guide on this journey. Of course, we have people who are looking to cheat us of our money or simply to waste our time—and we definitely need to be careful about them. More commonly, however, we might encounter people who haven't been on the journey themselves or who haven't done the majority of the work required to achieve self-actualization. Such people might not mean to cause harm, but they can seriously disrupt our journey through their misguided advice. So, it makes sense to take the reins of our spiritual journey in our own hands.

There's another reason why this is important. Ultimately, this journey is all about understanding ourselves at a deeper level and connecting with the Universal Consciousness. It's about strengthening our intuition and allowing ourselves to listen to our inner voice. No matter who we choose as our mentor, we're the only ones who can truly guide ourselves home.

In this chapter, we'll gain a deeper understanding of the spiritual awakening journey and also learn about the things to keep in mind as we begin our own journey.

The Difference Between Knowledge and Knowing

Ever since the advent of the internet, knowledge seems to have become more accessible to people around the world. It's so much easier today to expose ourselves to different cultures, learn about different ways of living, and gain knowledge about things we would otherwise have no idea about. This, of course, is a boon. The problem is that most people tend to stop at this level. More importantly, most people don't even know that there are any more levels to reach on their journey.

When it comes to spiritual enlightenment, different schools of thought are united in one aspect: There's a difference between knowledge and knowing, and this difference can affect our spiritual journey. Simply put, knowledge is about acquiring information from different sources. For some people, the concept of knowledge itself is very limited. They might restrict themselves to gathering information on topics that they're already familiar with. Some might even have trouble entertaining any point of view that challenges their own beliefs. Others might use the limited knowledge they have to put others down or to dictate terms to others. This is why we might see people who are experts in their fields or who have years of experience behind them behaving in an unkind manner to others. This is because they don't want to test the limits of their ignorance.

Some people are truly dedicated to the pursuit of knowledge, and it's their love for knowledge that allows them to understand and respect different opinions. They aren't drunk on knowledge, nor do they keep flaunting what they know to others. In fact, they're more than willing to work with people who are just starting out and who are keen on learning. These people have stepped into the realm of knowing. They're interested not only in acquiring information but also in making sense of that information with an open mind.

What, then, is true knowing? Knowing is all about *realization*. When we process information from our surroundings, we don't do so to tell ourselves that we're gaining knowledge. Instead, we want to engage deeply with that information. We want to grow and expand our horizons. Most importantly, we want to understand what it is all about. We're not satisfied with the superficial or the convenient. In fact, we're suspicious of it.

The subtle difference between knowledge and knowing has been discussed in various schools of thought. In Islam, we have two words that highlight this difference—*'ilm* and *'irfan*.

While *'ilm* means knowledge, especially knowledge that can be interpreted in much the same way by anyone, *'irfan'* is recognition. This means that *'ilm* has to do with textual and material knowledge, while *'irfan* has to do with deep spiritual knowledge, which is unique to an individual.

According to ancient yogic philosophy, there's a difference between the various kinds of knowledge and the state of knowing. That which is known as *shastra gyan* (knowledge of texts) can make someone learned but not wise. *Gyan* (knowledge) has to do with the material world, while *bodh* (realization or enlightenment) is related to the absorption of experience. This experience doesn't have anything to do with formal teaching and everything to do with how open we are to the worlds around and within us.

How do you know whether someone's pursuing knowledge or knowing?

- The one who's pursuing knowledge might get irritated when they encounter something challenging. The one who's after knowing is more than eager to deal with challenges. In fact, they might even welcome them.
- A seeker of knowledge will usually not go beyond the superficial aspects of something. Think of someone who likes collecting trivia. They might get excited at the prospect of "knowing" a lot of things, and they usually have an arsenal of facts at their disposal. However, there's a good chance that most of them don't have an in-depth understanding of most of the topics they know about. A similar thing happens in life.
- Knowledge is largely material in nature, while knowing is all about spirituality. You might have all the knowledge in the world without knowing anything.

- People who only seek knowledge usually "don't know that they don't know." People who pursue knowing always "know that they don't know."
- The pursuit of knowledge is, by its very nature, focused outward. The pursuit of knowing is focused on our inner journey.
- Knowledge is usually about finding the most convenient answer, while knowing is about sitting with the most uncomfortable questions.

There's another interesting aspect to the differences between knowledge and knowing. The pursuit of both knowledge and knowing can be lifelong, but knowledge doesn't necessarily lead to wisdom. In fact, knowledge for knowledge's sake can make us feel empty—and not in the spiritual sense where it is imbued with meaning. Knowing, on the other hand, helps us meet our true selves. In fact, true knowing can feel like an emptying of our individual sense of self—more commonly known as our ego—in order to become indistinguishable with the Divine Consciousness.

Wisdom is a complex attribute—one that combines knowledge, intuition, insight, and experience—that helps us navigate life in a way that is true to us. Of course, wisdom needs to be earned, which is why people believe that the older we get, the wiser we become. However, it's not quite as simple as that, is it? As we've discussed earlier, we might sometimes feel like we're blocked from accessing the wisdom of the world, no matter how experienced or knowledgable we are.

Those who don't know what they're missing out on are still okay, as their ignorance protects them in a way. However, those who have felt the stirrings of something they cannot quite comprehend—and who know that there's more to life than what they've seen or experienced on the physical plane—are the ones who are about to embark on a journey that is both challenging and rewarding. This is known as the journey of spiritual awakening.

What Is Spiritual Awakening?

The difference between knowledge and knowing is important because the spiritual awakening process is what helps you bridge the gap between the two. In fact, in many cases, you might even have to abandon one path to be able to truly pursue another.

As we've discussed before, spirituality has become an overused—if not abused—concept these days. That's not to say that more people becoming spiritually-inclined is a bad thing. However, when a concept becomes popular without proper reflection both by the people who espouse it and who adopt it, there's a chance that it will stray away from its original meaning. In this section, we'll discuss what spiritual awakening is, and what are some of the things to keep in mind if you're undergoing this process.

Spiritual awakening is a process that leads to a shift in your understanding and consciousness. This brings about a change in how we see the world and ourselves, and helps us align our lives to the truest version of ourselves. I understand that this definition might seem lofty and unattainable, but you needn't be intimidated by its scope.

Let's first look at some common signs and symptoms of a spiritual awakening:

- **A sense of unease or longing**: If your life looks perfect on the outside and you still feel like you're missing something, there's a chance that you need to pay attention to your spiritual self. This can happen in two scenarios. You might be someone who has always felt a little lost and ill-adjusted to this world. Or, you might have always been able to navigate this world easily and things have suddenly changed for you. If you feel a longing for something that you cannot quite put your finger on, it could be an indication that you need to go within yourself.
- **Questioning things that you've taken for granted**: The conventional way of the world asks us to "settle" as soon as possible—to find a rhythm for our lives that we can follow for as long as possible. This is why any form of uncertainty can unsettle us. When you start your spiritual awakening process, however, you might start questioning many aspects of your life. For example, you might begin to take a closer look at your relationships and ask yourself if they are truly healthy. Or, you might start examining your work more closely and ask yourself if it brings meaning to your life. You might not receive the answers you need immediately, but the questions will often set you on a path where you can change something you're not aligned with anymore.
- **Heightened awareness and intuition**: You might suddenly find yourself more attuned to the world around you. Many things that you didn't notice earlier start to become evident to you. Your senses might seem more awake, and you might be picking up on energies and auras of those around you. These qualities are always present within us but they become sharper during a spiritual awakening.

- **Shift in breathing patterns**: As we ease into our awakening process, we tend to become calmer. This also shows up in our breathing patterns. Our breathing becomes slow and relaxed, allowing us to feel more peaceful and deeply connected with the universe. During this process, our parasympathetic nervous system gets activated, which works contrary to the sympathetic nervous system. Your body and mind then move from a "fight or flight" mode to a "rest and digest" mode.
- **Developing a sense of devotion**: Spiritual awakening can cultivate a sense of devotion within us. You might find yourself devoted to a Divine entity or a way of life, but you might also begin a new practice or strengthen an existing practice. Often, this period can bring a renewed sense of inspiration and creativity. You might feel like putting these heightened sensibilities to good use by creating art. You might also experience the elusive "flow" state when you're working on something. For example, you might lose track of time and completely immerse yourself in your practice.
- **Becoming more mindful in your life**: Spiritual awakening helps us connect deeply with the present. We begin to be more grateful for what we have now, rather than worrying about the future or feeling sad about the past. You might find yourself enjoying the little things in your present, and having more appreciation for the seemingly mundane moments that make up your life. Contrary to what many people might think, this isn't about becoming "boring" but about opening yourself up to the wonder in little moments.
- **Embracing meaningful solitude**: In general, humans are scared of being alone. Sure, there's a lot of beauty in connecting with people, forming communities, and finding our place in the world. However, when we

surround ourselves with others in order to avoid facing ourselves, we're using our relationships as a crutch. When we begin to appreciate the gift of solitude, we become comfortable with meaningful silence, and we want to spend as much time as possible getting to know ourselves. In the beginning, we might have to spend a lot of time alone to heal ourselves. Even when the process is over, we might find ourselves wanting to set aside some time to deepen our relationship with ourselves.

- **Accessing deeper states of meditation**: If you're already into meditation, you might start noticing that your practice has become stronger during this time. You might be able to meditate longer and the quality of your meditation might also improve. For those who aren't into meditation, you might start to get interested in it. When it comes to meditation, there are a few things to keep in mind. In the beginning, it's a good idea to follow an expert on meditation, either offline or online. It's also a good idea to check in with your doctor and ask them if you should be practicing meditation. This is especially important because when we start accessing deeper states of meditation, it can be an unsettling experience if we're already dealing with mental health issues. We'll discuss some of the meditation techniques that can help you with your third eye chakra awakening process in the next chapter.
- **Becoming aware of the interconnected nature of the universe**: The ego is present to protect us from the world. Therefore, it creates a sense of "us versus the world" within us. This is why we might go through the world feeling disconnected with ourselves and others. We might also feel like an insignificant cog in the cosmic wheel. The spiritual awakening process often comes with an experience of ego dissolution. During this process, all

the walls that we've constructed begin to fall down and we begin to experience the interconnectedness of the universe. This concept is also illustrated through Indra's net, a metaphor for the perfect interconnectedness of all things in the universe. This concept is popular in Hindu, Buddhist, and Taoist schools of thought. According to the concept, there is a large net that hangs over the palace of Lord Indra. Each vertex of this net has a jewel embedded in it, and every jewel of this net can be reflected in all the other jewels. In the same way, we are the jewels whose luster depends on all the other jewels of the world. Spiritual awakening helps us become aware of this fact.

- **A renewed sense of purpose**: You might be the most ambitious person in the world and still feel unfulfilled. This is because our ambition might not be equivalent to a purpose that makes life worthwhile for us. For example, you might want to earn a certain amount of wealth by a certain age. Or, you might want to buy a house or get a coveted position in your organization. None of these ambitions are frivolous if they make sense to your life. At the same time, you might feel empty even after achieving these goals. If you find yourself "looking for more" from life, you might be moving toward a phase of spiritual awakening in your life. Often, people find their true calling during this phase. For some, this purpose might be entirely different to what they thought they would be doing in their lives. For others, their purpose could be related to a field they already work in, but they might be compelled to look at it in a different way.

- **Detachment from the material aspects of life**: It's important to note here that you don't need to completely give up on money or material pursuits during an awakening process. Detachment doesn't mean running away from something. Instead, it means that you don't allow yourself to be defined by your material possessions. Your focus shifts from the material aspects of your life to more spiritual pursuits. Your material pursuits—the ones that are essential for you—will become a means to an end rather than an end in themselves.

- **Questioning your relationships with others**: For many people, this period can be extremely isolating mainly because they don't feel understood by others. Apart from this, they might need to do a lot of work in solitude, which can put a strain on their relationships. However, the most striking aspect of this phase is that it tests our relationships to a great extent. For example, you might find yourself noticing certain issues in your relationships that you might otherwise have ignored. Or, you might become more aware of relationships that are mostly one-sided in nature. During this time, you might even lose certain relationships that you thought were going to last a lifetime. This can be confusing and upsetting, but look at it in another way. Whatever is meant to last will remain in your life and you will eventually end up with genuine connections that honor your authentic self.
- **More powerful dreams:** Our dreams already hold a lot of power over our lives, but we might not be aware of this all the time. During a spiritual awakening, our dreams can become our companions—walking with us, guiding us, and making us aware of the possibilities in our waking life. Some people can experience a lot of signs and synchronicities in their dreams. Others might even experience lucid dreaming. A lucid dream is basically a dream that you have while being aware that you're dreaming. So, you're not awake, but you're

conscious enough to witness your dream as it unfolds. While you might experience a lucid dream without any effort—as many do—you can also induce a lucid dream through certain techniques (more about this later). Many people believe that lucid dreams are a powerful form of manifestation, and they're more commonly experienced by people who are undergoing an intense spiritual awakening.

- **More intense emotions that can swing between extremes**: During this time, you might experience intense emotions of all kinds. As I've mentioned before, you might experience anger and frustration when you first undergo a third eye chakra awakening. Similarly, you might even be reminded of certain unpleasant experiences in your life that you thought you had healed from. This is a way for our consciousness to purge itself of anything that could be holding us back from experiencing true bliss. At the same time, you might experience periods of intense happiness and love. You might be able to forgive people from your past and let go of old wounds. You might even get a taste of unconditional love—not only toward your loved ones but also toward yourself as well as strangers. Of course, there might be instances of you going from a "high" state to a "low" state without any apparent reason. This can be extremely difficult to deal with, but it's all part of the process.
- A spiritual awakening—as rewarding as it is—can be extremely challenging for us. Even though the term has become more popular over the years, not everyone goes through a spiritual awakening, which can make it all the more isolating and confusing. Many of us worry about whether we're doing things right, or if we'll be able to deal with all the changes that such an intense experience

brings. It's easy to listen to people perpetuating myths in the name of spiritual guidance. Therefore, let's go through a few things that we should keep in mind when it comes to the journey:

- **There's no right or wrong way of being on this journey.** Sure, there are a few points that can help you in the form of guidance, but there are no hard-and-fast rules. We often waste too much time obsessing over details that should or shouldn't be part of this journey. The truth is, a spiritual awakening brings you closer to the truest version of yourself. By definition, then, no one else can tell you what you should or shouldn't be doing on this path. This is where your intuition comes into play. The more you work on getting in touch with your intuition, the more confident you'll become of following your own path. Another thing to understand is that spirituality goes beyond the notions of "right" and "wrong." Your spiritual journey should only feel right to you.

- **It can take a long time for us to rise above the tendency to rationalize this journey.** See, our thoughts are how we make sense of the world. We form opinions, analyze things, and try to make the most rational decision possible. Even when we're "following our heart," we're actually begging with our head to listen to our heart. This is completely understandable. It's how we can exist in a world that places a lot of emphasis on logic and reason, even when we know that human beings are *really* rational creatures. This journey, then, can be a huge jolt to our consciousness. We might suddenly have to deal with experiences and events that cannot be easily explained. We might feel compelled to judge ourselves and others, but we can also see how judgment doesn't really help on this journey. For many of us, this creates a sort of limbo where we cannot let go of our rational selves but we also want to embrace this newer version of ourselves. All I can say is, give it time. It will be a while before you can observe your thoughts without judgment and lean into the journey.

- **This journey happens in Divine timing**. For those who are just starting out on the journey, this concept can sound absurd and even frustrating. Human beings have extremely strong willpower, which is why we're used to exercising it in every aspect of our lives. There's nothing wrong with this, and willpower certainly plays a role in how our lives shape up. However, when we start believing that things will only happen according to our will, we prevent ourselves from enjoying the blessings that can only come from the Divine will. It's natural to get impatient once in a while, but understand that you're on this path to try and understand things that are beyond your perception and control. This also applies to things like the initiation and duration of this process. For some people, this process occurs as a result of various lifestyle changes and consciously choosing a more spiritual path. For others, it might happen without any conscious efforts at all. Similarly, some people might have a short period of awakening, while for others, it might go on for years. These things don't depend on the time you've spent on something as much as on the kind of karma you've accumulated (more on this in the seventh chapter). The important thing is to go where the journey takes you.

- **Comparison is the thief of joy, love, and awakening**. The thing is, a spiritual awakening can make you seem like you're "the chosen one." Since it's not extremely common and it can certainly be transformative, it's hard not to think of ourselves as *special*. Once we start doing that, however, we're treating this sacred process in the same way that we treat many of our interactions in the physical world. For example, we might see this as a race against others who are also on the spiritual path. We might feel frustrated because someone else has reached a certain stage in their process that we haven't. We might also feel like other people are having an easier time with their process. The thing is, comparisons are bad anywhere, but especially in this process. Your personal journey cannot be measured against someone else's journey. Don't take away from the joy that you can experience on this journey by doing so.

- **Mistakes are a part of the journey**. I would even say that mistakes make the journey more meaningful. If you're not making mistakes, what are you learning? This journey can also bring up a lot of embarrassing memories in which we are reminded of our past mistakes. It's not easy to see all our flaws and be kind to ourselves, but this is exactly what we need to do if we want to experience unconditional love and joy. If you cannot love yourself in spite of the mistakes you make, you'll never be able to love someone else. More importantly, the awakening journey isn't about achieving perfection. It's about becoming comfortable with whoever you are. Each mistake that we make tells us something about ourselves, and it's extremely important to embrace these mistakes as lessons.
- **If you're not okay with who you are today, you're not going to be okay with your "awakened" self**. This might run counter to the concept of spiritual awakening we're familiar with. After all, don't we embark on this journey because we want to change something about our lives, or because we feel like something's missing? Sure, but there's a difference between wanting more from our

lives and being unkind to the current version of ourselves. You can improve and try to elevate yourself spiritually without disparaging who you are now. This is important because if we don't learn to accept and love ourselves unconditionally for who we are today, we're only chasing a distant version of ourselves that isn't even guaranteed. This is a sure shot recipe for distress and disappointment. Another reason why this is important is that a spiritual awakening does not always lead to the kind of transformation we're promised by some gurus. In fact, there's a good chance that your life will look pretty much the same as before even after the journey. So, what changes during this process? If we're receptive to it, we're going to gain wisdom and intuition that helps us navigate life in an authentic way. We're going to learn to accept life as it comes and enjoy what we have today without worrying about what we don't. This can be the hardest lesson to learn for most of us.

- **There's no destination to this journey.** For some of us, this journey occurs in phases that might be separated over months or even years. For others, it could happen in one phase. Either way, this journey doesn't really end for anyone who has embarked on it. We're always learning more about ourselves. In fact, once we've reached a certain level of perception, we might find that there's a lot more work to do. This can seem discouraging, but only if you want to "get it over with." This journey is all about joy, and learning to appreciate the journey is proof that you're becoming more evolved spiritually.
- In this chapter, we've tried to understand the meaning of true knowing, intuition, and spiritual awakening. In the next chapter, we'll discuss certain practices that can help awaken your third eye chakra.

Chapter 5
Practices That Can Help Align Our Third Eye Chakra

As we've discussed earlier, there are various ways in which we can align our third eye chakra. In this chapter, we'll look at certain lifestyle practices that can help us during the process.

Diet and Third Eye Chakra Alignment

According to yogic traditions, our diet plays an important role in our spiritual practice. In general, a plant-based diet is supposed to be more in alignment with these practices. There are a few reasons for this. All yogic practices—including chakra alignment—are related to our internal energies. So, it's important that these energies are light and balanced. When our energies become heavy, it can be difficult for them to move around our subtle body. This can also create blockages during the practice.

In Ayurveda, food is classified into three main categories based on their effect on our energies—*sattvic*, *rajasic*, and *tamasic*. In general, rajasic and tamasic foods should be eaten in a limited manner if we want a strong yogic practice. This is because rajasic foods are those that produce excess energy in the body. This energy can easily manifest as restlessness, irritability, anger, sleeplessness, and hyperactivity. As we've seen, anger, irritability, and sleeplessness can block our third eye chakra. Not only that, but these books can lead to toxicity in the blood and also make us feel heavier. Some examples of rajasic foods are

- Artificially flavored and preserved foods
- Sour milk and cream
- Fried foods
- Foods roasted with salt
- Foods with lots of mustard
- Foods that have strong flavors, such as garlic, vinegar, onions, pickles, chilies, and certain pungent vegetables
- Chocolate
- Alcoholic drinks
- Carbonated drinks
- Coffee
- Foods that are extremely sour, salty, or spicy
- Foods containing meat and fish

Tamasic foods are on the opposite end of the spectrum. They bring lethargy and inertia to our bodies and minds. When we eat foods that are tamasic in nature, we can feel lazy, uninspired, confused, and even disoriented in some cases. What's more, if we eat tamasic foods in combination with rajasic foods, we also risk increasing the aggressive qualities of rajasic foods. Some examples of tamasic foods are

- Artificially flavored and preserved foods like jams and jellies
- Hard liquor
- Chips, french fries, and excessively salty foods
- Foods with excess starch

- Canned and tinned foods
- Foods high in saturated fats and added sugar
- Refined sugar
- Refined flour
- Milk, curds, and cheese that are either highly pasteurized or kept in very cold temperatures
- Stale food
- Foods containing meat and fish

As you can see, there's a fair bit of overlap between rajasic and tamasic foods. While foods rich in animal products are a part of the list, so too are foods that are prepared and preserved artificially and those that are extremely high on flavor.

The best diet for anyone who is trying to cleanse their chakras using yogic practices is a sattvic diet. Sattvic foods are those that are light and moderate in taste. They emphasize freshness and purity, and they are free from any artificial preservatives. Since these foods are natural and light, they help energize us and also restore our prana. Some examples of sattvic foods are

- Fresh fruits and fruit juices
- Fresh vegetables—especially leafy greens that are boiled or cooked in moderate spices—and fresh vegetable juices
- Nuts and seeds that are eaten fresh or after roasting lightly (these should be eaten in moderation)
- Sesame oil, olive oil, and coconut oil
- Grains such as brown or wild rice, wheat, oats, and different kinds of legumes
- Fresh milk, buttermilk, yogurt, butter, and ghee

- Raw sugar, honey, and jaggery for sweetening our foods
- Fresh spices such as turmeric, coriander, ginger, cardamom, cinnamon, and fennel

As you can see, for a sustained yogic practice, we need to be energetic and balanced at all times. This is usually possible through a sattvic diet. Foods that are rich in animal products can be heavy for these energies. Similarly, heavily processed foods are usually high on refined sugar, salt, and saturated fats. They also contain chemicals and foreign substances that our bodies are not used to. All of this can create an imbalance in our subtle energies. Even if you follow a nonvegetarian diet, make sure that you're consuming products that are fresh and that come from animals who have not been subjected to confinement and cruelty.

There's another reason to deeply consider the foods you have on a regular basis when undergoing a spiritual awakening. The process of awakening usually involves a lot of "karma clearing." Simply put, this is a process where we try to deal with the consequences of our past actions. Since eating meat goes against the concept of *ahimsa* (non-violence), most yogis in the original tradition refrain from it. In general, anything that might mess with your energy and make it harder for you to cleanse your chakras need to be avoided.

My suggestion would be to pay close attention to how different foods affect you. You can keep a food journal in which you note down the foods you consume and the moods you experience during the day. For example, you can note down if you've been feeling unusually lethargic during the day. Or, you can make note of the feelings of lightness that you experience on certain days. Try to look for patterns between your diet and your mental and physical health. Once you start your yoga practice, you'll be able to observe these effects more intensely. For instance, you might find that a certain kind of food schedule disrupts your yoga practice, while another helps to strengthen it. You might also start noticing how certain foods affect your senses. Once you're aware of the effects of different foods on your body and mind, you can cut down on those foods that disrupt your journey and increase the intake of foods that help you on the way.

Once we reach an advanced stage of our journey, we should also look at our attachment to food. In other words, once we have a fair idea of which foods to eat and which to avoid, we should spend a lot of time and energy on deciding what to eat in our daily lives. This doesn't mean that we stop enjoying our meals. In fact, we might experience more enjoyment from simple meals than we did before. The thing is, we need to move away from an obsession with material aspects of our lives as they keep us locked in lower states of awareness.

Another reason why we should not be overeating during this time is because too much food slows down our internal processes. Our digestive system depends on the *jatharagni* (digestive fire) for proper metabolization of food. When we eat a lot, this fire weakens and makes us feel lethargic. There are different kinds of fire within us, some of which are related to our intellect and intuition. When the digestive fire weakens, our subtle energies are engaged in promoting digestion rather than in stimulating our intuitive abilities.

While it's important to eat mindfully and in moderation, don't worry if this seems impossible in the beginning. The more conscious we become, the easier it will be to naturally move away from these behaviors.

Now that we've discussed what our general diet should look like, let's see if there are certain foods that can help us specifically on the third eye chakra awakening journey.

Foods That Help Us on Our Third Eye Chakra Awakening Journey

The third eye chakra is closely associated with our pineal gland. Since the pineal gland is related to our circadian rhythms and melatonin levels, we can focus on eating foods that help regulate these levels. Some of these foods are tart cherries, goji berries, nuts, and warm milk. If you consume milk products, you can also eat eggs and oily fish like sardines and salmon.

Another way of looking at this is by paying attention to the color associated with the third eye chakra. Since the color is indigo, we should focus on foods that are dark blue or deep purple in color. Some of these foods are

- Purple-colored variations of vegetables like kale, cabbage, broccoli, carrots, potatoes, and beans
- Eggplants
- Plums
- Raw cacao
- Purple grapes
- Purple figs
- Prunes
- Dates

- Blackberries
- Raisins

Also, since this chakra resides in the head, we need foods that are good for our brain. For example, nuts, seeds, dark chocolate, and oily fish are rich in antioxidants and in omega-3 and omega-6 fatty acids. These foods help the brain function properly and improve our focus and stamina. Acai is also a superfood that is usually helpful in balancing our third eye chakra energies. In terms of herbs, you can add lavender, dill, juniper, rosemary, star anise, valerian, and thyme to your foods and drinks.

The Importance of Yoga in Third Eye Awakening

If you have followed health and fitness trends in the recent past, chances are, you're aware of the popularity of yoga. In the west, yoga is usually associated with physical health and wellness. Of course, a consistent yogic practice can help immensely in improving your balance, fitness, and energy levels. It can also be instrumental in improving our mental and emotional health. However, few people know that yoga originated as a deeply spiritual practice. In fact, the word yoga comes from the Sanskrit word *yog* (or *jog*), which means "to unify." Here, the aim is to achieve ultimate unity between our consciousness and the Universal Consciousness. As you can see, this aim is very similar to our aim of awakening the third eye chakra.

Yoga is much more than a fitness regimen or a mindful movement practice. It's a way of life, and we need to deeply understand the principles behind it if we want to use it as a spiritual practice. In this section, we'll discuss some principles of yoga that can help us align our third eye chakra, and we'll also learn about some practices that we can do on a regular basis.

When you're starting out in yoga, you should seek a good teacher, especially because things like posture and proper techniques are extremely important here. If you keep practicing the wrong way, you might end up causing serious harm to yourself. Also, since yoga is a powerful form of working with your prana, you need to pay attention to how your body and mind reacts to these techniques.

There are other things to keep in mind while practicing yoga. If you're practicing yoga in the morning, make sure you're on an empty stomach. If you're practicing it in the evening, try to have a gap of at least four to five hours between your last meal and your practice. This is very important. Also, you need to check in with your body throughout the practice. It's perfectly normal to experience soreness when you're first starting out, or even when you resume your practice after a break. However, you should not be experiencing any sharp pains during this time. If you do, you should immediately stop your practice and consult a doctor. If you already suffer from pain in your back or joints, you should first ask your doctor if it's okay for you to practice. Even if they approve, you need to be cautious during your practice.

For people who menstruate, it's usually okay to practice when you're on your period. However, if you experience pain or discomfort during this time, please refrain from practicing for the duration of your period. Also, certain *asanas* (yoga poses) are prohibited during this time, so keep that in mind.

As you can see, it's immensely helpful to have a dedicated teacher during the first few months of your practice. Remember: Don't compare your journey with someone else's. For one, all of us have different flexibility levels—what seems easy to someone else might not be easy for you. That's okay. Yoga is about getting in tune with *yourself*, so have patience during the journey. Most importantly, remember that even the best and most enlightened guru can only show you the path. Only you can do the work required to awaken your third eye chakra. Lastly, yoga—like any other practice—only shows results when you're committed to it. So, take some time, but try to incorporate it into your lifestyle for good.

Let's now discuss some effective yogic practices that can help with third eye chakra awakening.

Yoga Asanas for Third Eye Chakra Awakening

The most effective yoga asanas for third eye chakra awakening are those in which we need to focus intensely on a point, or which gently stimulate your forehead or third eye.

Balasana (Child's Pose)

This is a pose that helps ground ourselves and also promotes calmness. It can also be a great way to relax between more strenuous asanas. It's known as the child's pose because it signifies how a child might like to rest. While it's a deeply relaxing pose, there are some things to be kept in mind while practicing it.

To get to this pose, you need to first go into the *table pose*, in which your knees are placed directly under your hips and on the ground and your hands are directly below your shoulders. Your palms and feet lie flat on the ground. Now, from this pose, you slowly move into the child's pose. For this, you need to slowly move your hips to your heels, while at the same time touching your forehead gently to the floor. Your toes should be touching each other. Your knees can either be together or slightly apart, based on your comfort level. Try to keep your palms, elbows, and feet firmly planted on the mat and keep your spine elongated without making it too rigid. While you're doing this, you need to exhale slowly as well. This is important because your body is contracting at this time.

Once you reach this position, take a few deep breaths while keeping your belly tucked in. Only do this for as long as you're comfortable, after which you can gently raise yourself up by using your palms and sitting on your heels. When you move from the child's pose to the seated position, make sure you're inhaling slowly and deeply.

A few things to keep in mind during this practice are:

- Don't do this pose if you're suffering from knee issues, as it can place a lot of strain on your knees.
- If you cannot comfortably touch your hips to your heels or your forehead to the ground, don't strain and put yourself at risk of injury. Instead, use cushions or yoga blocks under your hips and forehead until your body becomes flexible enough.
- Remember to breathe at all times. It can take some time for your breaths to sync with your moves, and that's

okay. Just remember to consciously breathe whenever you can.

This is a great pose to help relieve tension in the neck and back and to stimulate your digestive processes. It can help relieve muscular tension in the whole body. Since this is a powerful grounding technique, it can help you become calm and can also recharge you for the next part of your practice or the rest of your day. If you're dealing with a lot of stress, anxiety, or fatigue, this is a great pose to practice.

Since this is the child's pose, it's a great way to connect with our own inner child. Our inner child is a part of us that often goes neglected as we try to navigate the adult world. This part of us often carries the codes for the traumas and joys we've experienced as a child. It also carries many subconscious aspects of ourselves that can tell us more about our hopes and dreams. When we talk about connecting with and healing our inner child, we're trying to get in touch with the aspect of ourselves that was more intuitive than our adult selves. This pose also applies gentle pressure to the *bhrumadhya* (center of the eyebrow), which is considered as the place where the third eye chakra resides.

Ardha Pincha Mayurasana (Dolphin's Pose)

This is another pose that gently stimulates the *bhrumadhya* and helps with third eye chakra awakening.

To do this pose, you start with the table pose as before. From the table pose, you need to exhale and lower your elbows so that they touch the floor, and your forearms should be on the floor as well. Your palms should be spread out in front of you and should be shoulder-width apart.

Next, you need to raise your hips so that they point upward. Use the strength of your arms to do so. Your feet should be hip-width apart and your heels should be placed firmly on the floor.

Your back needs to be straight and your shoulders shouldn't be scrunched up. In other words, there shouldn't be any tension in your neck and shoulders. How will you know if you're holding the position properly? You should feel a deep stretch in your hamstrings if your hips are positioned properly and your back is straight. This pose is similar to *adho mukha svanasana* (downward-facing dog), except that your elbows and forearms are on the ground. So, when you look at yourself in the mirror—which is a good way to practice as a beginner—you should be able to see the shape of a mountain being formed by your back, hips, and legs.

While the ideal position requires that your knees are locked, you can bend them a little as a beginner if it's difficult for you. The important thing is to keep your back straight. Once you've attained this position, you can let your forehead gently touch the floor and take a few breaths there. After this, slowly exhale and come back to the table top position. You can even go down to take the child's pose if you want.

Some scenarios in which you should not take this pose are

- If you suffer from glaucoma.
- If you've been diagnosed with hypertension and aren't taking any medicines for it.
- If you've suffered an injury in your back, arms, or shoulders.

In the first two cases, you need to get an approval from your doctor regarding your eligibility to practice.

Apart from aligning our third eye chakra, this pose is great for building upper body strength, stretching our spine and hamstrings, and releasing any tension in our back and shoulders. If you want to stimulate your third eye chakra even further, you can bring your palms together in *anjali* mudra (*namaste* sign) under the *bhrumadhya*. Then, take both thumbs and press them gently on your *bhrumadhya*. This will intensify your practice.

Garudasana (Eagle Pose)

This is a standing pose that might require quite a bit of balance when you're starting out. Don't worry, though: You'll soon get the hang of it. The best way to begin this pose is by grounding ourselves firmly through the practice of *tadasana* (mountain pose). In *tadasana*, you need to stand straight. Then, take one foot and place it perpendicular to the other foot. This is done to ensure that you have a one-foot distance between both your feet. Now, make sure that the pressure on both your feet is equally distributed. You should not be experiencing excess pressure in any one area of your feet. Once you feel stable and grounded, stretch your palms as they face outward. Your fingers should be pointing downward. Take a few deep breaths in this position.

After this, you need to bend both your knees a little. Your right foot is firmly placed on the floor, while your left foot crosses over your right foot. How do you do this? Make sure your left thigh is placed over your right thigh. At this point, your left shin should be loosely placed in front of your right shin. You now need to twist your leg such that your left shin now goes behind your right shin and your left foot is locked firmly around your right shin with the toes pointing downward. It can take some time for you to do this properly. Don't strain yourself while doing this.

Once you feel a sense of balance, stretch your arms in front of you such that they are parallel to the floor. Then, cross your left arm over your right arm and bring this formation to a position that is perpendicular to the floor. At this point, the palms of both your hands should be facing away from each other. Then, turn your palms so that they face each other and bring them together. Once you can hold this posture, you need to stretch your fingers upward.

Your *drishti* (gaze) should be fixed directly ahead of you. Hold this position for as long as possible while breathing deeply. When you're ready to release this posture, first untangle your hands and place them at your sides. Then, gently untangle your left leg from your right leg and come back to tadasana. Stay in that posture for some time before you take a rest.

This posture can seem a bit complicated in the beginning, but all it needs is dedicated practice. It also has immense benefits. For example, it can help improve balance and increase flexibility, especially in the hips and legs. It can also stretch different parts of your body, such as your thighs, hips, upper back, and shoulders. Since it requires a fair bit of strength and flexibility of the legs, it can also help strengthen your calf muscles over time. For those of us who suffer from rheumatism or sciatica, this pose can be immensely helpful if done in the right way. Of course, this pose should not be practiced by anyone who has suffered injuries in the ankles, knees, or elbows.

When you start doing this asana, you'll notice that it requires a lot of focus to do it properly. This focus is what makes it a great asana for strengthening our third eye chakra.

Apart from these beginner-friendly poses, there are a few other poses that can help with third eye chakra activation. These are *paschimottanasana* (seated forward bend pose), *upavistha konasana* (wide-angle pose), and *shirshasana* (headstand pose). As I've mentioned earlier, it's a good idea to start these poses under the supervision of a trusted teacher. Also, don't expect to be perfect immediately. It will take some time, but if you learn to breathe into your body, you'll enjoy the journey a lot more than you think.

In this chapter, we've learned about the lifestyle practices that can help awaken our third eye chakra. In the next chapter, we'll learn about some other techniques that can help us sharpen our intuitive abilities.

Chapter 6
Practices to Strengthen Your Intuition

To understand how truly powerful our intuition is, let's understand what happens when the third eye chakra awakens. The third eye chakra has been described as an "internal screen" of our consciousness. Through our physical eyes, we see physical images that help us make sense of the material world. Through the third eye, we see images and memories that are beyond the perception of our physical eyes. This is where intuition and imagination come into play. People who have achieved a level of mastery over their third eye chakra can display a wide range of abilities, such as

- **The ability to interpret dreams and visions**: We've talked briefly about lucid dreaming in the fourth chapter. An awakened third eye chakra opens up our consciousness to various dreams and visions. We can now look at these dreams in depth and attach meaning to them.
- **Enhanced psychic abilities**: If you've ever seen a psychic on a television show, you must have seen how they suddenly receive a vision and then provide information to others based on that vision. In real life, psychic abilities are related to extrasensory perception (clairvoyance), which deals with the ability to perceive what cannot be seen or felt by our worldly senses. Some

people are able to glimpse into the past to recognize a pattern or clue that could help them in the present. Others are able to see something that is not commonly known or is deliberately hidden from public view. In this way, they provide information in the form of images.

- **Telepathic abilities**: The word "telepathy" translates to the ability to perceive another person's feelings and thoughts through a distance. In other words, you can sense what the other person is going through even when you're not explicitly communicating with them. This is also a sign of enhanced intuitive abilities.

- **Astral projection**: Astral projection refers to the ability to have an "out-of-body" experience. What does this mean? When our consciousness elevates to such a level that it's capable of leaving the physical plane for an extended period of time, it allows us to traverse this plane without being attached to it. While some people can experience this phenomenon without any conscious effort, most people induce this phenomenon through third eye chakra awakening.

- **Aura perception**: Even without the third eye chakra awakening, you might have noticed certain "vibes" emanating from people. Some people give off very strong vibes, which means that anyone can pick up on their energies. Others have muted energies, but some people are still able to discern these vibes. People who have an awakened third eye chakra have such strong intuitive abilities that they can sense the "aura" of people. An aura is basically an energy field that surrounds a person. Our aura can change due to the situation we are in and the people we interact with. Some people have a malleable aura, meaning it can be changed easily. Others have a somewhat fixed aura. Usually, people with an awakened third eye chakra can "see" their own as well as other people's auras. They can thus check in with themselves and others based on what they sense. In some cases, these auras can be also seen in the form of colors that stand for various moods and emotions. Those who are able to perceive auras also realize that every living object—and some non-living ones—possess a vibration that is unique to them. Being able to tap into these vibrations helps us move through the world in a highly conscious manner.

- **The ability to experience true happiness**: The third eye chakra is all about the dissolution of worldly barriers. These barriers can be found within ourselves as well as in our interactions with others. A great barrier to happiness is the perspective that highlights the differences in the world. Once the third eye chakra is awakened, you're able to see the truth of this world and embrace everyone in the same spirit. Also, you're able to embrace your true self, which means that there's no longer any conflict within yourself. Contrary to the popular belief of having to "chase happiness," you'll be able to experience it deep within yourself. This kind of happiness is not temporary, nor can it be threatened by anything external to us.

When people talk about the third eye chakra, they usually talk in terms of the amount of power that we now have access to. This is certainly true, for a heightened intuition can be immensely powerful. However, this power isn't to be understood in the same way as worldly power. This power is related to ultimate mastery over our own self. Apart from these abilities—which aren't guaranteed to everyone—how do you know if your intuition has become stronger and your third eye chakra is in the process of alignment?

Signs of Heightened Intuition

What happens during this process? How do you know that your intuition is becoming stronger? While there are physical symptoms to look out for, the strongest signs could be related to the cognitive, emotional, and behavioral changes you see within yourself. Let's look at some of these symptoms:

- **You might experience a tingling sensation in the region**. When your chakras align, a lot of energy exchange takes place. This can sometimes feel like a tingling sensation in the physical area which corresponds to the chakra.
- **You will become more neutral in your observations of others**. This change will be more apparent if you're usually an opinionated person. You'll see that you can now hold back from expressing emotions or opinions that are too extreme in nature. This doesn't mean that you don't express anger, dissatisfaction, or happiness when it's required. All it means is that you won't rush to judge yourself and others, and that you practice a certain level of detachment from your emotions.
- **You'll become responsive to people and situations instead of reacting to them**. When we're overwhelmed by our emotions, we tend to react sharply to situations and people. If—during a difficult situation or conversation—you find that you can step back, pause, and then formulate a response, you've likely matured energetically.
- **You'll want to help people**. When we feel aligned with ourselves, we want to extend the peace and happiness we feel to others around us. By itself, spiritual awakening doesn't have a lot of meaning. In fact, some of the most enlightened people in the world tell us that a truly awakened soul goes through life discharging their duties

in much the same way after the process is over. So, how does an awakened soul make a difference? They help others in any way possible. They don't think too deeply about their powers and their "elevated status," but pay attention to ways in which they can create a positive influence on other people's lives. The true mark of an awakened soul, then, is their ability to think beyond themselves.

Issues Faced During This Process

When we're trying to strengthen our intuition, we can run into some problems during the process. Let's look at some of these in detail so that we can work on them:

- **Illusions of any kind**: In yogic philosophy, this world is often referred to as *maya*, which stands for illusion. This is often used to explain how the material aspects of this world are not real. You might have heard different variations of this, such as, "We're all living in a simulation" or "The whole world is nothing more than a dream conjured up by the creator." The aim is not to reject the whole world as an illusion, but to find something real within this simulation. As long as you hold on to beliefs that are not true—or to people who don't share something real with you—your intuitive abilities are going to be blocked.
- **Obsessions and confusion due to too much energy in the third eye chakra**: Just as too little energy in the third eye chakra can make us feel blocked, too much energy can make us feel obsessed, overwhelmed, and confused. This chakra offers us the power of visualization and perception. However, too much energy in this chakra can make us see visions that overpower us.

In extreme cases, we might even have to deal with hallucinations, nightmares, and delusions.
- **Difficult emotions like anger, frustration, and fear**: To be clear, the problem doesn't lie in experiencing these emotions. In fact, these emotions are usually an indication that we're on the right path. The problem lies in the fact that many of us become demotivated when we're faced with these emotions. Spiritual awakening processes can be extremely taxing. Also, if you have to go through this process while also dealing with your worldly responsibilities, it can be challenging even on the best days. If you have to deal with difficult emotions on a regular basis, you might want to give up on the process entirely.

How Can We Strengthen Our Intuition?

Before we discuss the various practices that can help deepen our intuitive energies, let's talk about the duration of the process. There's no rule that says your third eye chakra should be awakened in a particular amount of time. In rare cases, this process happens almost spontaneously and so can be completed in a very short span of time. In most cases, however, this is a process that can take months or even years. For many, the awakening process is equivalent to a lifetime of practice.

The thing is, you need to be patient with yourself if you want to get anywhere during this process. Also, it's a common misconception that you need to cast aside your responsibilities and regular duties if you want to experience an awakening. All you need is sustained practice. Even if you can spend 15–30 minutes each day on an intuitive practice, you'll find yourself progressing much faster than you expected. What's most important is that you try to work on your intuitive abilities throughout the day. By this, I mean that, no matter what you do, try to live a life that honors your intuition.

Also, you need to remember that the third eye chakra can only be aligned when our lower chakras are in balance. So, during this process, you cannot neglect their health as well. If your emotions get the better of you—or if you resort to unhealthy practices—your lower chakras might get blocked and challenge the entire process. In fact, if you're somehow able to align your third eye chakra but your lower chakras are blocked, you might not even be able to handle it in a healthy manner.

Most importantly, don't try to force any of your chakras to align. If you're unclear about your reasons for pursuing a third eye chakra awakening, or you try to speed up the process through drugs or the advice of so-called gurus, you'll be doing a lot of harm to yourself. As we've discussed before, when there's too much energy in your third eye chakra and you don't know how to handle it, you might have to deal with complex mental and emotional issues.

The Use of Essential Oils

Essential oils are basically oils that are extracted from plants. They're highly concentrated and can impact our health in various ways. While many people swear by the benefits of essential oils, it's important to remember that these formulations aren't regulated by the Food and Drug Administration. This means that we don't have a standardized process of testing these oils for safety and efficacy. Also, different people can have completely different reactions to the same oil. So, you need to do your research before you start using a certain oil on a regular basis. Make sure you're convinced about the quality of these oils and the reliability of the manufacturers who produce them. Additionally, essential oils can cause allergic reactions on some people's skin. So, before you use them for the first time, always conduct a patch test on your skin. Last but not least, remember that certain essential oils can be sensitive to light. So, it's a good idea to not go out into the sun after applying these oils.

Essential oils have many benefits. For example, they can help relieve pain and tension in various areas of our body. Their fragrance can also calm our nerves, improve our mood, and help us sleep better. Some people believe that certain essential oils can help in stimulating the pineal gland, which is closely related to the third eye chakra. The best oils for this are lemon, sandalwood, and jasmine. Other essential oils that can be used during this process are juniper, frankincense, rosemary, patchouli, German chamomile, and marjoram.

To make an essential oil blend for third eye chakra alignment, you need to first choose a carrier oil to go with your essential oil. This is because essential oils are highly concentrated and they shouldn't be applied directly on our skin. The carrier oil dilutes the essential oil without diminishing its efficacy. Some examples of carrier oils are jojoba oil and coconut oil. To make the blend, take one teaspoon of the carrier oil and mix it with six drops of the essential oil. After conducting the patch test and ensuring that the blend is safe for application, apply it directly on your *bhrumadhya*. You can even chant the bija mantra "Om" or any affirmation of your choice during this process.

Meditating With Crystals

Crystals are commonly used for healing and energy work. This is because people believe that these solids are capable of holding energy within themselves. Each crystal has a unique vibration that corresponds to certain qualities. These crystals can be powerful, so we should be careful while using them. Since the color associated with the third eye chakra is indigo, it's recommended to use crystals that are indigo, violet, blue, and purple. An example of such a stone is tanzanite, which can help heal the third eye chakra and also help strengthen our intuition. Similarly, sodalite is another such crystal that helps deepen our intuitive abilities. Some other crystals that can be used are

- Iolite
- Purple sapphire
- Sodalite
- Rhodonite
- Fluorite
- Celestite
- Labradorite
- Amethyst
- Citrin
- Black obsidian
- Purple-violet tourmaline

Third Eye Meditation Techniques

Meditation of any kind is extremely powerful for our spiritual awakening. That being said, third eye chakra meditation should focus more on the *bhrumadhya* as well as on the power of light.

The Practice of Sun Gazing

The concept behind sun gazing is that natural sunlight is one of the most powerful sources of light that can stimulate the pineal gland and the third eye chakra. So, some people espouse the practice of intently gazing at the sun for a few minutes during sunrise and sunset. This is said to heal the third eye chakra and strengthen our intuitive abilities. However, medical experts caution against this practise because they don't recommend anyone to look directly at the sun. It can cause serious and even permanent damage to our eyes.

So, what can you do instead? You can practice this meditation while sunbathing. For this, you need to sit in the sun either during sunrise or sunset. As you do that, you can close your eyes and imagine that the sun is shining where your *bhrumadhya* is located. You can simply imagine a yellow ball of light on your *bhrumadhya* and focus your attention on it for some time.

While it's best to do this practice in natural sunlight, you might be living in an area where you don't get a lot of it. In that case, you can invest in artificial lights that are warm and yellow in color.

Trataka Dhyana (Gazing Meditation)

This is a great practice that can help you in multiple ways. *Trataka* means "to gaze." During this meditation, we need to pick an object that we will gaze at, and use it to improve our focus as well as align our third eye chakra. While this meditation is safe for most people to practice, children and people with preexisting eye conditions should avoid it.

In this practice, we'll be using the flame of a candle or *diya* (Indian earthen lamp). For a powerful experience, it's advisable to switch off the lights in your room or to sit in a darkened room if practicing during the day. The best time to practice this meditation is in the morning, but you can do it whenever you have 10-15 minutes to spare. Once you're seated in a comfortable position, place the *diya* or candle at a distance of 1–1.5 meters from your eyes. The flame should be at eye level. Then, you can close your eyes for a second before you look intently at the flame in front of you. Do this for as long as you can without blinking. In the beginning, this will be a bit uncomfortable, but don't panic. Gaze at the flame only as long as you can. Then, as you begin to close your eyes, imagine that you're taking the flame and placing it on your *bhrumadhya*.

Spend some time meditating on the image of the flame till you're ready to gaze at the actual flame again. Repeat the process as long as you can. Once you start getting used to this process, you'll be able to hold your gaze for longer periods of time. Experienced meditators hold their gaze till their eyes begin to water.

This is a meditative practice that helps strengthen the connection between the eye, mind, and inner eye. Physically, it can help strengthen the eye muscles and even improve eyesight in some people. This practice can also improve our concentration and attention span over a period of time. Not only that, but it can also help reduce anxiety and help improve our sleeping patterns. Spiritually, this practice can help deepen our intuitive sense and awaken our third eye chakra.

Third Eye Chakra Visualization

Another simple meditation practice is related to the visualization of the third eye chakra. You can sit in a comfortable position as you imagine your third eye on the *bhrumadhya*. If you don't want to visualize an eye, you can even visualize an indigo-colored dot or circle on your *bhrumadhya* and focus your attention on it for a few minutes. Some people also like to visualize the word "Om" written on the *bhrumadhya*.

During the visualization, make sure that you are relaxed and that you're breathing as calmly and deeply as possible. Also, in the beginning, you might not be able to visualize clearly, or you might feel fidgety while doing the meditation. Some meditators also report that they start feeling a bit tingly in the third eye region when they start meditating. Don't worry about any of it. It'll take a while for you to become comfortable with this practice, and that tingling sensation might be an indication that your third eye chakra has started opening up.

Pranayama Techniques for Third Eye Chakra Awakening

Pranayama is an ancient yogic technique that helps us balance our prana through breathwork. In this section, we'll learn how to use pranayama to align our third eye chakra.

Before we learn about specific techniques, however, it's important to keep certain things in mind:

- **Be mindful of your diet**. The food you consume has a direct impact on your prana. Usually, a gap of three to four hours between your practice and your last meal should be maintained. The aim is to allow the food you've eaten to be properly digested without feeling hungry again. A sattvic diet is your best bet because it keeps your prana aligned and unencumbered.

- **Find a place that facilitates your pranayama practice.** If possible, you should try to do your practice outdoors. If that's not possible, choose a space within your house that is properly ventilated and allows the flow of natural air. This place should also be as free of external disturbances as possible.
- **Try to fix a time for practice and stay consistent.** As with any other practice like meditation and asana practice, it's always better to maintain a consistent schedule for your pranayama practice. The best time for any spiritual practice is the period before sunrise—also known as *brahma-muhurta*—because our *prana-shakti* (strength of our life force energy) is highest at this time. If you cannot set aside time in the morning, the next best time is around sunset. Most importantly, try to stick to the schedule that works for you as it will make it easier for your prana to align at that time.
- **Sit in a calm and stable manner.** As much as possible, keep your posture fixed without being rigid. In other words, you should not be fidgety while you practice pranayama. Try to stay calm and focus entirely on your practice. Remember that you need the prana to flow easily and steadily throughout your subtle body.
- **Your spine should be straight and your abdomen should be in a neutral position.** Your posture is instrumental in ensuring an effective practice. In yogic philosophy, there are three main *nadis*, which are *ida*, *pingala*, and *sushumna*. Ida is the left *nadi* which signifies Shiva, the logical and masculine energy. *Pingala* is the right *nadi* which signifies Shakti, the intuitive and

feminine energy. The *sushumna nadi*—which is the central *nadi*—is the one that is related to the merging of Universal Consciousness with Divine Consciousness. When the life force energy enters this *nadi*, we enter a state of *vairagya*, which means "beyond color." In a way, it is the ultimate peak of our spiritual capabilities and it is closely related to the third eye chakra awakening. If we want our subtle energies to be fully balanced, we need our prana to be able to enter the *sushumna nadi*. This can only happen if we keep our spine straight at all times. Also, as we learn to synchronize our breathing, our abdomen might also rise and fall along with the breaths. We need to ensure that our abdomen is as steady as possible during the practice.

- **Don't force your breaths at any time**. In the beginning, it might be difficult to synchronize your breaths as needed. That is okay. Remember that you're trying to work with your life force energy so you cannot force anything at any point. Try to stay relaxed as you learn these techniques.
- **It's a good idea to work with asanas before we start pranayama**. In yogic teachings, asana practice comes before pranayama. One important reason for this is that asana practice opens up our body, helps us stretch our muscles and spine, and increases flexibility in the body. It also helps to naturally correct our posture. All these things make it easier for the prana to flow through the body, so you should work on your asana practice before you start pranayama.
- **It's strongly recommended that you begin your pranayama practice under an experienced teacher**. As I've mentioned earlier, these techniques work with our prana and *nadis*. Our life force energy is extremely powerful, which is why it's important to know how to

channel this energy properly. If we don't follow the steps properly or if we make mistakes, there's a chance that we'll end up causing more harm than good to ourselves. So, it's a good idea to learn the proper techniques as well as the precautions to be taken before you start practicing independently.

Let's now look at a few techniques that you can practice to align your third eye chakra.

Nadi Shodhana Pranayama

Nadi shodhana stands for "the purification of energy channels or *nadis*." Through this technique, we can cleanse our energy channels of any stress or toxicity that gets accumulated over time. It's also a great way to get rid of any traumas that could have blocked our *nadis*. This technique is also called *anulom vilom*, or alternate nostril breathing.

Here are the steps for the *nadi shodhana* pranayama:

- Sit comfortably with your spine straight. Your left hand should be on your left knee, with your flat palm either open to the sky or in chin mudra. In chin mudra, the tips of your thumb and index finger gently touch each other.
- The tips of the index and middle fingers of your right hand should be gently placed on the *bhrumadhya*. This will stimulate the third eye chakra.
- Next, you should place the tips of the ring and middle fingers on your left nostril, while your thumb is placed on the right nostril. Here, we use the respective fingers to alternately open and close the nostrils while we inhale and exhale.

- First, you use your thumb to close the right nostril as you gently and deeply exhale through the left nostril.
- Then, inhale deeply and gently through the left nostril and then place your ring and little fingers on the nose to close this nostril.
- After this, open the right nostril by removing the thumb from the side and gently exhale through it.
- Now, inhale from the open right nostril and then close it by placing your thumb on the nostril. Then, exhale from the left nostril by removing the two fingers placed on it.
- This sequence of inhale (left), exhale (right), inhale (right), exhale (left) is known as one round of *nadi shodhana*. Try to complete at least ten rounds of the same. Keep your eyes closed throughout the practice.
- There are a few things to keep in mind during this particular practice:
- When I talk about nostrils, I mean the part of the nose that is close to the nostrils. You don't have to place the fingers on the openings themselves.
- Breathe only through your nose. Do not use your mouth to inhale or exhale. Also, don't take *ujjayi* breaths, which is when we breathe more deeply than usual and it causes a slight constriction at the base of our throat.
- The fingers should be gently placed on both your nose and forehead. Do not apply any unnecessary pressure.
- In the beginning, this practice might make you feel a bit tired. Give it time, as your prana is aligning itself within your subtle body. Also, make sure that the time you take to exhale is longer than the duration of your inhale. This can also help combat lethargy after the practice.

- In the beginning, you need to simply exhale and inhale without any holds. After you're comfortable with this practice, you can even introduce the practice of holding your breath between inhales and exhales.

Bhramari Pranayama

This technique is also known as the "bee breath." It refers to the buzzing sound made by a bee. Here are the steps that you need to follow:

- Place both hands on your face as you seat yourself in a comfortable position.
- Your middle fingers should be placed over your eyes, your index fingers over your eyebrows, and your ring and little fingers just under the cheekbones.
- Once you've done this, use both your thumbs to close your respective ears.
- Inhale deeply through an *ujjayi* breath. For this, you have to close your mouth and take a deep inhale through your nose so that you can feel a slight constriction in your throat.
- As you exhale, make an "mmmm" sound with your mouth closed. It should resemble the buzzing sound that a bee makes.
- Try to do this practice for two to three minutes at one time.

This is a great practice for improving circulation within the body and for enhancing our intuition and awareness. If you suffer from low blood pressure, you should not be practicing *ujjayi* breathing. Also, make sure that you're always doing this exercise in the upright position.

Yogic Breathing

This is the simplest pranayama technique that can be done by anyone without the supervision of a guru. All you need to do is focus on your breathing as you take deep and gentle inhales and exhales. You can start by doing this for five to ten minutes in the beginning, and then extend it as per your comfort. Try to keep your exhales longer than your inhales. This helps relax your body without making you feel sleepy or fatigued.

If you have trouble sitting still—or if you would prefer to be more active during this process—you can try *active yogic breathing*. In this technique, you do the same practice while walking. If you can walk outdoors, you'll get the added benefit of being close to nature during this practice. Try to take ten steps for each inhale and exhale. Of course, if you can take deeper and longer breaths, all the better. However, don't force yourself to keep inhaling or exhaling at any time. This is also a great technique to calm yourself down when you're feeling agitated, nervous, or angry. Simply walk off your emotions while breathing deeply, and you'll notice that you feel more balanced almost instantly.

Once you become adept at your asana and pranayama practice, you can combine various techniques for maximum benefit. In the beginning, however, it's a good idea to focus on only one pranayama at a time so that you can learn it properly and not cause harm to yourself.

Hakini Mudra

We've discussed the significance of this mudra in the second chapter. Remember that this is a *hasta* mudra so we need to learn how to use our hands properly. Let's now learn how to practice this mudra for third eye chakra awakening:

- First, your palms should be facing each other and have a small distance between them.
- Now, touch the tip of each finger and thumb of one hand with that of the corresponding fingers and thumb. The tips should gently touch one another and not be tightly pressed together.
- You can bring this hand formation to the level of your forehead and keep it close to the *bhrumadhya*.
- Then, start inhaling and exhaling deeply while keeping your focus on the *bhrumadhya*.
- When you inhale through your nostrils, your tongue should touch the roof of your closed mouth. When you exhale, your tongue should be relaxed as usual.
- This is a great practice to start your day with, but you can do it any time throughout the day. Usually, you should set aside 30 minutes for this practice. If you find that you cannot do this practice in a single 30-minute stretch, you can split it into sessions of 5–10 minutes throughout the day.

Dream Journaling

We've discussed earlier how our dreams can provide important clues related to our spiritual path. Not only that, but they can also help us live our lives better on the physical plane. As our third eye chakra practice deepens, our dreams usually become more vibrant and significant. When this starts happening, it can be both confusing and overwhelming to us. This is because we might feel like we're getting signs from everywhere but we cannot make sense of them. It's a bit like when someone frantically speaks to you in a foreign language. You *know* they desperately want to communicate with you but you cannot understand them, try as you might.

Also, dreams can have a wide range of interpretations. The same symbols can be interpreted in different ways depending on the context. This means that your life experiences, issues, and expectations all play a role in the kind of dreams you have. When we keep a dream journal, we do two things. One, we tell ourselves that our dreams are important and that we're willing to pay attention to what our intuition is telling us. Two, we understand exactly what our dreams tell us and use this powerful knowledge to live a life that is aligned to the truest version of ourselves.

What are some things you should keep in mind when you start keeping a dream journal? Keep your journal and a pen as close to you as possible. This is because it's best to note down your dreams just after you've had them. If you wake up suddenly and find nothing close to you, you might forget the essential details by the time you can write them down. While you can also take notes on your phone, it's best to use a dedicated journal for this so that you can properly read through it like the story of your life.

Try to be as detailed as possible. Write down the things that seem most significant to you first, then add any other details you can think of. Even if your dream is hazy, write down whatever you can remember. What's important is that you're consistent with this practice. Also, experts suggest that you write down the time and date of the dreams as well. This can help when you're trying to form patterns related to these dreams.

Get into the habit of reading your journal weekly. This way, you can start forming narratives in your head regarding all these dreams. You might find surprising connections between seemingly disparate dreams and come to conclusions that you might otherwise have missed.

One thing you can do to make this practice much more powerful is to ask yourself questions related to these dreams. Instead of simply writing down the dreams, ask yourself what they could mean. Is there a particular need or expectation in your waking life that is not being met? Do these symbols mean something specific to you? Are these signs indicating any changes that need to be made in your life? Are there any particular obstacles that you're currently facing in your life? When you answer these questions honestly, you'll be able to make the most of the signs and symbols you come across in your dreams.

Last but not least, have patience with yourself while you do this practice. You cannot expect to get all the answers in a short amount of time. After all, you're peeking through layers of your subconscious mind to understand what your third eye is trying to tell you. It's going to take time. Even if you don't understand things in the beginning, write them down. You never know when they might start making sense.

Harnessing the Healing Power of Nature

We talked about alpha waves in the second chapter. These waves are emitted when we are calm and relaxed, open and intuitive. The brains of children emit these waves. As we grow older, the frequency of these waves reduces, making it difficult for us to connect to our intuition. One of the easiest and most effective ways to increase the frequency and intensity of alpha waves in our brains is by connecting deeply with nature. It's true that most of us live our lives surrounded by towers of concrete. However, we should actively seek out green spaces close to us. If possible, we can also take short hikes across wooded trails located close to where we live. The more time we spend in nature, the easier it becomes for us to awaken our third eye chakra and deepen our intuitive abilities.

Other Techniques to Awaken Our Third Eye Chakra

Apart from the practices mentioned above, there are a few simple things you can do in your daily life to ensure that your intuition becomes sharper over time:

- **Dedicate yourself to a passion**. You don't need to change careers or find a new job to do this. Even if everything else remains the same, take out some time during the day to dedicate yourself to something you enjoy doing. This could be related to music, dance, art, or even something more academic or technical. The nature of the activity doesn't matter as long as you're able to lose yourself in it completely. Remember how an activated third eye chakra can improve our focus? Well, the opposite of this is also true. If you can focus intensely on something that brings you joy, your third eye chakra will awaken more easily.
- **Try a visual detox**. The third eye chakra is closely related to our physical vision. On a daily basis, we are bombarded with images and visuals from all directions. While we cannot completely limit what we see, we can place certain controls on it. For example, if you're used to binge-watching entire series at a time, try to limit

yourself to one episode a day. Similarly, if you're in the habit of scrolling through social media sites looking at images of other people—images that are usually a distorted representation of their real lives—you should try to cut down your consumption of these images. See, our third eye chakra is aligned when we see things for what they are. This clarity is marred by the overabundance of false images in our life. So, you need to actively try to control what you see and how it affects you.

- **Try something new and question your old beliefs.** When your third eye chakra starts to awaken, you start questioning whatever you've taken for granted. The opposite is also true. As you start questioning your old beliefs and prejudices, your chakra awakens. If you want to replace judgment with curiosity in your life, try something new, meet people you normally wouldn't hang out with, and question your assumptions as much as you can.

- **Face at least one fear that you've held onto for a long time.** What is fear? It is our response to uncertainty. When we fear something, we're usually trying to desperately hold on to something else. This "something else" might not be beneficial for us, but it keeps us safe in the sense that we're firmly rooted in a reality we understand. For example, when we don't try applying for that new job that might expand our horizons, we're scared of leaving behind the job that might not do much for us. Why? Because a known evil always seems to be a safer bet in this volatile world. When we do this, however, we give away our power to fear. Fear blocks our intuition, which means that we cannot hear our inner voice or we dismiss it. So, try to select one fear that you've been meaning to overcome for a long time. How about taking that first step today?

In this chapter, we've discussed numerous techniques that can help strengthen our intuition. In the last chapter, we'll discuss the importance of chanting when it comes to the awakening process.

Chapter 7
The Importance of Chanting for Third Eye Chakra

There's a deep connection between sound and spirituality. In fact, each chakra corresponds to a certain bija mantra, the chanting of which can enhance our spiritual practice.

The Importance of Bija Mantras

The concept of bija mantras is related to ancient yogic and tantric thought. The word bija stands for "seed." Therefore, these mantras help us uncover our potential and bloom to become our truest selves. These mantras represent different vibrations of the universe, which is why they have a powerful impact on our chakras. Each chakra has a specific mantra attached to it. When we chant these mantras with intention, we unlock the power of the corresponding chakras.

It's important to remember that these mantras are extremely powerful, so we shouldn't use them without intention and purity of thought. Similarly, it's important to pay attention to their pronunciation and repeat them often to harness their true power.

Following are the bija mantras associated with the activation of each chakra:

- Root chakra: Lam
- Sacral chakra: Vam
- Solar plexus chakra: Ram
- Heart chakra: Yam
- Throat chakra: Ham
- Third eye chakra: Om
- Crown chakra: Silence (or silent Om)

The Significance of "Om"

Ancient gurus believed that "Om" is the most powerful sound in the universe. It is said to be the sound of creation of the universe. This is also a sound related to our inner self and to the Universal Consciousness. In fact, it's believed that all beings in the Universe vibrate with the energy of the Divine. This vibration corresponds to the bija mantra Om. When we keep chanting this mantra, we move beyond the intellect into something much deeper. Thus, it carries the energy of intuition.

The word "Om" is pronounced as "Aum"—as in, "Aaaa-uuuu-mmm"—when we use it for awakening the third eye chakra. Each of these three sounds corresponds to different states of consciousness. For example, A stands for the waking state, U stands for the dream state, and M stands for the state of deep sleep. Thus, the chanting of this mantra takes care of the entire range of consciousness that we experience.

Benefits of "Om" Chanting

Here are a few benefits of chanting "Om" during your practice:

- **This mantra is great for calming ourselves.** When we're feeling extremely stressed and anxious, this mantra helps us calm down and reach a state of peace within ourselves.
- **The three parts of the mantra help activate the different chakras.** Here, A stands for the heart chakra, U stands for the throat chakra, and M stands for the crown chakra. Another school of thought believes that A stands for the solar plexus chakra, U for the heart chakra, and M for the throat chakra. Either way, this one mantra helps to activate three different chakras at once.
- **It connects us both to ourselves and to others.** When we chant this mantra, our third eye chakra awakens, opening us up to the most authentic version of ourselves. This also helps us connect authentically and deeply with others. We become more compassionate, understanding, and loving by chanting this mantra.

How to Do a Chanting Meditation

Here are the steps you need to follow when doing an "Om" meditation:

- Sit comfortably in a quiet location, and make sure your back is straight.
- Bring your awareness to the third eye chakra and imagine the "Om" symbol written there.
- As you focus on this chakra, start chanting the mantra mentally or aloud—whatever makes you feel comfortable.
- Repeat this chant for at least 5–10 minutes in the beginning.

Another variation of this technique focuses on the three syllables: A, U, and M. In this method, you need to visualize each syllable as emanating from the corresponding chakra. For example, as you say "Aaaaa," you need to focus on the solar plexus chakra. When you say "Uuuuu," your focus shifts to the heart chakra, and as you say "Mmmmm," it shifts to the throat chakra. This way, all three chakras are energized along with the third eye chakra.

The Power of Affirmations

When you're working on your intuitive abilities, you'll likely witness your doubts resurfacing from time to time. It can be extremely difficult to stay on the path if you don't keep reaffirming yourself. This is why—in addition to Om chanting—we should also practice affirmations for our third eye chakra. Some examples of such affirmations are:

- I am blessed with clear vision and I can see everything for what it is.
- I am at peace with myself.
- I have achieved balance within myself, and this will create harmony in my material life as well.
- I trust my intuition and am open to receiving its wisdom and guidance.
- I am capable of living my life according to the guidance of my inner voice.
- I am going to follow the path that aligns with my truest self.
- I am aware of my own energy as well as the energies of those around me.
- I accept whatever comes my way because I'm always connected to the Universal Consciousness.
- I am always focused, attentive, and able to make good decisions.

- I am willing to explore new ideas and perspectives, even if they challenge my current beliefs.

You can start with these affirmations, and you can even add some of your own as you progress on your journey.

You can also use music as a way to activate your third eye chakra. In general, instrumental music is more effective than music with words. This is because it allows us to focus on ourselves rather than on the lyrics. Also, it's important that we listen to music only to relax ourselves and as inspiration to create or meditate. It's perfectly okay if we use music as a medium to escape, but it can come in the way of the activation process. So, we need to strike a balance between soulful sounds and silence in order to align with our truest selves.

Making the Most of This Journey

Before we move to the conclusion, there's one thing that we need to be aware of when it comes to this journey. The third eye chakra—by its very nature—awakens us to the reality of this world. While there are amazing aspects to this process, it's also true that we can now see through the many illusions that make up this world. In other words, there's a serious chance that we find ourselves disillusioned on this journey *because* of our ability to see through maya.

How do we combat this? After all, we don't want to lose our zest for life or start believing that everything is pointless. We don't want to lull ourselves into inactivity because the material world is a lie. The only way to make the most of this journey in a healthy manner is by becoming more playful.

In many Hindu traditions, there's a concept of *leela* or *lila*. *Leela* refers to the divine play that many gods and goddesses engage in. In fact, it's also believed that the universe is the result of *leela*. Through this perspective, we begin to see things not as tricks but as games. Admittedly, it's not easy for us to cultivate this attitude.

So, what can we do? We can try to find ways of experiencing joy in our daily lives. Seek out chances to meaningfully connect with others and enjoy yourself. Look for activities that you can do both alone and with others. Don't think too deeply about the utility of these actions. In fact, look for those activities that your "inner child" would enjoy. Think of the ways in which you can emulate a childlike response to this world.

After all, children are usually more intuitive than most of us, but that doesn't stop them from fully engaging with this world, right? Instead of retreating from the world, embrace it fully and experience all that it has to offer.

Conclusion

Even as the Western world becomes more familiar with the concept of spirituality and chakras, many people struggle to incorporate these teachings into their daily lives. When it comes to the concept of the third eye chakra, it might seem even more intimidating. After all, this is the second to last chakra and the last one that can be accessed through a conscious spiritual practice. Since it's so closely related to the Universal Consciousness, it can also seem sacred to the point of being exclusive. This is why many people might believe that third eye chakra awakening is not for them.

On the other end of the spectrum are those who want to experience everything that comes with an awakened third eye chakra, but don't always have the proper knowledge and guidance needed for the same. So, they try a lot of things and end up nowhere. Even if they make progress, they're often confused and overwhelmed—which is not how this process should feel like. In the absence of proper resources, such people might become frustrated and weary of the entire concept.

As I started learning more about these processes and the concepts behind them, I realized that this path doesn't have to be complicated or scary. In fact, if we keep in mind a few principles—and remember to check in with ourselves regularly—we're going to experience the multiple benefits of this path without exhausting ourselves out. Therefore, I wrote this book to help others approach this concept without fear and apprehension. I hope that, after reading this book, you'll have gained enough confidence to start your third eye chakra awakening journey.

Let's briefly go through some of the concepts that have been discussed in this book:

- In the first chapter, I gave a brief overview of chakras and briefly discussed each of the seven chakras. The aim was to help those who hadn't been introduced to chakras before this book, and also to explain the entire journey as a whole. As we've discussed throughout the book, it's important to work your way through the chakras in sequence. Only when your "lower" chakras are balanced should you begin work on your "higher" chakras.

- In the second chapter, we familiarized ourselves with the third eye chakra. We discussed the color, element, and mudra associated with it. Also, we learned about the various spiritual traditions that embrace the concept of the third eye chakra. In this chapter, we also looked at how science deals with this concept.

- The third chapter was all about understanding the symptoms of a blocked and an aligned third eye chakra. We discussed all the different ways in which our physical, mental, emotional, and spiritual health can be affected if our chakra is blocked. Similarly, we discussed the benefits of a balanced third eye chakra.

- In the fourth chapter, we delved deep into the concepts behind knowing, intuition, and spiritual awakening. We understood the distinction between knowledge and knowing. We also envisioned how spiritual awakening can look like for us. In addition, we discussed the things to keep in mind while going through this journey.

- The fifth chapter helped us familiarize ourselves with the lifestyle changes that can help awaken our third eye chakra. We looked at the diet practices that can elevate our journey, and also at the various yoga asanas that can help strengthen our intuition.

- In the sixth chapter, we discussed the signs of heightened intuition. We also understood the difficulties that we might face when we're going through this process. Then, we discussed numerous ways to strengthen our intuition and activate our third eye chakra. These include essential oils, crystals, third eye meditation techniques, pranayama, and mudras. Apart from this, we also discussed other techniques like dream journaling, spending time in nature, and facing our fears.

- In the seventh chapter, we talked about the importance of bija mantras and chanting during third eye chakra meditation. We understood the benefits of "Om" chanting, the power of affirmations, and the best techniques for chanting meditations.

I hope this book has given you valuable information that you need on this journey. I also hope that it has made you less intimidated at the prospect of taking your first steps. Most importantly, I hope that this book has given you the courage to live a more authentic, aware, awakened, and joyous life.

My friends, I request you to leave a review on Amazon if this book has inspired you in any way. This will hopefully help the book reach many other readers like yourself who might benefit from reading it. Thank you for reading and take care.

Thanks for reading!

I'd greatly appreciate it if you took just a moment to leave an honest review on Amazon. If you don't have the time to leave a review, a simple rating will work just fine. Every bit helps.

Thank you for your support!

Also, don't forget your **FREE** gift! Just scan the code below.

References

A brief introduction to Tratak meditation. (2023, July 26). Art of Living (India). https://www.artofliving.org/in-en/meditation/meditation-beginners/tratak-meditation

Agna chakra – Clarity beyond color. (2018, January 20). Isha Sadhguru https://isha.sadhguru.org/in/en/wisdom/article/agna-chakra-clarity-beyond-color

Ajna (third eye) chakra: Meditation, powers, mantras, benefits. (2022). Rudra Centre. https://www.rudraksha-ratna.com/articles/ajna-chakra

Ajna chakra – The third eye chakra. (2014, January 13). Sanskriti - Hinduism and Indian Culture Website. https://www.sanskritimagazine.com/ajna-the-third-eye-chakra/

Anziani, M. (2021, August 20). *Activate your chakras by chanting the bija mantras.* Yoga Journal. https://www.yogajournal.com/live-be-yoga-featured/activate-chakras-with-bija-mantras/

Ashby, G. (2017, March 22). *Religion & culture | 'The third eye': A gateway to psychic powers.* (2017, April 2). The Gleaner. https://jamaica-gleaner.com/article/news/20170402/religion-culture-third-eye-gateway-psychic-powers

Ashish. (2021, February 2). *Preparation for pranayama: Importance & useful guidelines*. Fitsri. https://www.fitsri.com/articles/preparation-for-pranayama

Atmabodh or self-realisation. (2015, June 17). India Travelogue. https://www.indiatravelogue.com/sacr/refl/atmabodh.html

Burgin, T. (2023, March 7). *Spiritual awakening: Definition, signs and symptoms*. Yoga Basics. https://www.yogabasics.com/connect/yoga-blog/spiritual-awakening/

Camacho, N. A. (2021, December 12). *Keeping a dream journal can unlock the power to your subconscious—Here's how to do it*. Well+Good. https://www.wellandgood.com/dream-journal/

Child's pose (Balasana): Instructions, tips & benefits. (2023, January 4). Yoga Basics. https://www.yogabasics.com/asana/child/#:~:text=Balasana%20is%20composed%20of%20two,child%20in%20a%20resting%20position.

Clarke, G. (2022, December 9). *Chakra foods: What to eat to balance the seven chakras*. The Yoga Nomads. https://www.theyoganomads.com/chakra-food/

Dillof, S. (2008, February). *Ishvara pranidhana: The power of surrender*. Jivamukti Yoga. https://jivamuktiyoga.com/fotm/ishvara-pranidhana-power-surrender/

Dolphin. (2013, November 7). Yoga Basics. https://www.yogabasics.com/asana/dolphin/

Everheart, D. (2023, July 14). *The comprehensive guide to understanding and balancing your 7 chakras*. Art of Living (United States). https://www.artofliving.org/us-en/meditation/chakras/chakras-guide

Foster, J. (2015, June 17). *10 simple principles of spiritual awakening*. Ekhart Yoga. https://www.ekhartyoga.com/articles/practice/10-simple-principles-of-spiritual-awakening

Garudasana - Eagle pose. (2021, December 8). Art of Living (India). https://www.artofliving.org/in-en/yoga/yoga-poses/garudasana-eagle-pose

Gheban, B. A., Rosca, I. A., & Crisan, M. (2019). The morphological and functional characteristics of the pineal gland. *Medicine and Pharmacy Reports, 92*(3), 226-34. https://doi.org/10.15386/mpr-1235

Groff, R. (2021, September 24). *Exploring your intuition: The third eye chakra*. Midtown Yoga. https://midtownyogastudios.com/blog/third-eye-chakra

Hailey, L. (2022, November 28). *What is the third eye? Science + spirituality of the third eye chakra*. The Yoga Nomads. https://www.theyoganomads.com/third-eye-chakra/

Himalayan Yoga Institute. (n.d.). *9 yogic breathing practices for mind-body balance and healing*. Retrieved August 9, 2023, from https://www.himalayanyogainstitute.com/9-yogic-breathing-practices-mind-body-balance-healing/

Hughes, A. (2020, June 3). *5 benefits of chanting Om*. Yogapedia. https://www.yogapedia.com/2/6010/meditation/om/the-5-benefits-of-chanting-om

Indigo color psychology and meaning. (2015, August 21). Color Psychology. https://www.colorpsychology.org/indigo/

Jain, R. (2020, October 7). *Third-eye chakra: Your guide to awakening the ajna chakra.* Arhanta Yoga. https://www.arhantayoga.org/blog/ajna-chakra-your-third-eye-chakra-awakening/

Karlsen, K. (2023, July 20). *Chakra sounds: A comprehensive guide.* Vocal Medicine. https://kathleenkarlsen.com/chakra-sounds#:~:text=Chakra%20Sounds%20and%20Bija%20Seed%20Syllables,-Each%20of%20the&text=The%20seed%20syllables%20for%20the%20seven%20main%20chakras%20are%20as,basic%20role%20of%20each%20chakra.

Kristin. (2022, February 13). *Third eye chakra: Everything you need to know.* Be My Travel Muse. https://www.bemytravelmuse.com/third-eye-chakra/

Kumar, R., Kumar, A., & Sardhara, J. (2018). Pineal gland— A spiritual third eye: An odyssey of antiquity to modern chronomedicine. *Indian Journal of Neurosurgery, 7,* 1-4. https://www.thieme-connect.com/products/ejournals/pdf/10.1055/s-0038-1649524.pdf

LeMind, A. (2012, June 2). *The third eye in culture and science.* Learning Mind. https://www.learning-mind.com/third-eye-mysteries-and-reveals/

Mishra, P. (2020, December 7). *Bhagavad Gita — Atam gyan.* Medium. https://runjhun-gold.medium.com/bhagavad-gita-atam-gyan-96058b2c6924

The pineal gland & the eye of Horus. (n.d.). Ophthalmology Breaking News. Retrieved August 9, 2023, from https://ophthalmologybreakingnews.com/ophthalmologynews-the-pineal-gland-the-eye-of-horus#google_vignette

Pizer, A. (2022, October 1). *What is the third eye (Ajna chakra)?* Verywell Fit. https://www.verywellfit.com/what-is-the-third-eye-3566789

Rindner, G. (2021, February 20). *Yes, astral projection is real, but* Behind Her Eyes *doesn't paint the full picture.* Oprah Daily. https://www.oprahdaily.com/life/a35550715/what-is-astral-projection/

The secrets of third eye activation & how it transforms your life. (2022, December 30). Art of Living (India). https://www.artofliving.org/in-en/meditation/secret-of-third-eye-activation

Seeing beyond the physical: The third eye chakra. (n.d.). Wisdom Tree Yoga. Retrieved August 9, 2023, from https://wisdomtreeyoga.com/news/seeing-beyond-the-physical-the-third-eye-chakra/

Snyder, S. (2021, May 5). *What you need to know about the Ajna chakra.* Yoga Journal. https://www.yogajournal.com/yoga-101/chakras-yoga-for-beginners/chakratuneup2015-intro-ajna/

Stelter, G. (2023, February 13). *A beginner's guide to the 7 chakras and their meanings.* Healthline. https://www.healthline.com/health/fitness-exercise/7-chakras#Chakra-101

Stokes, V. (2023, March 16). *How to open your third eye chakra for spiritual awakening.* Healthline. https://www.healthline.com/health/mind-body/how-to-open-your-third-eye

The story of Shiva's third eye and its hidden symbolism. (n.d.). Sadhguru. Retrieved August 9, 2023, from https://isha.sadhguru.org/mahashivratri/shiva/shivas-third-eye-its-hidden-symbolism/

Suwal, C. (2020, July 21). *What happens when you open your third eye?* Insight Timer Blog. https://insighttimer.com/blog/what-happens-when-you-open-your-third-eye/

The third eye chakra and its indigo color meaning. (2014, January 16). Color Meanings. https://www.color-meanings.com/brow-or-third-eye-chakra-the-sixth-chakra/

Third eye chakra healing with Om mantra - Lyrics, meaning, benefits, download. (n.d.). Mahakatha. Retrieved August 9, 2023, from https://mahakatha.com/mantras/third-eye-chakra-healing-with-om-mantra

Third eye quotes (96 quotes). (n.d.). Goodreads. Retrieved August 9, 2023, from https://www.goodreads.com/quotes/tag/third-eye

Three types of food. (2022, September 19). Art of Living (India). https://www.artofliving.org/in-en/culture/navratri/three-types-food

Tseten, L. M. (n.d.). *How to see with your third eye.* Kripalu. Retrieved August 9, 2023, from https://kripalu.org/resources/how-see-your-third-eye#:~:text=All%20the%20Buddhas%20have%20a,the%20wisdom%20eye%20is%20open.

The two ways to open the third eye. (2017, March 3). Sadhguru. https://isha.sadhguru.org/in/en/wisdom/article/two-ways-to-open-third-eye

Villines, Z. (2023, February 16). *What is the pineal gland?* Medical News Today. https://www.medicalnewstoday.com/articles/319882#pineal-gland-dysfunction

WebMD editorial contributors. (2020, October 30). *Foods high in melatonin.* WebMD. https://www.webmd.com/diet/foods-high-in-melatonin

What is hakini mudra? - Definition from Yogapedia. (2020, August 11). Yogapedia. https://www.yogapedia.com/definition/7614/hakini-mudra

What is nadi shodhan pranayama. (2023, January 31). Art of Living (India). https://www.artofliving.org/in-en/yoga/breathing-techniques/alternate-nostril-breathing-nadi-shodhan

Yogapedia Editorial Team. (2017, June 6). *3 reasons why yogis love plant-based diets.* Yogapedia. https://www.yogapedia.com/2/6724/yoga-practice/health/vegetarians-make-better-yogis

Printed in Great Britain
by Amazon